'Simply a Particular
Contemporary'

THE FRENCH LIST

'Simply a Particular Contemporary'

Interviews, 1970–79

Roland Barthes

Essays and Interviews,
Volume **5**

TRANSLATION AND

EDITORIAL COMMENTS

BY CHRIS TURNER

LONDON NEW YORK CALCUTTA

www.bibliofrance.in

The work is published with the support of the Publication Assistance
Programmes of the Institut français

Seagull Books, 2023

Compiled from Roland Barthes, *Oeuvres complètes* (Éditions du Seuil,
1993–2002).

© Éditions du Seuil, for *Oeuvres complètes*, *tome I*, 1993 and 2002
© Éditions du Seuil, for *Oeuvres complètes*, *tome II*, 1993, 1994 and 2002
© Éditions du Seuil, for *Oeuvres complètes*s, *tome III*, 1994 and 2002
© Éditions du Seuil, for *Oeuvres complètes*, *tome IV*, 1994, 1995 and 2002
© Éditions du Seuil, for *Oeuvres complètes*, *tome V*, 1995 and 2002

First published in English translation by Seagull Books, 2015
English translation © Chris Turner, 2015

ISBN 978 1 8030 9 278 2

British Library Cataloguing-in-Publication Data
A catalogue record for this book is available from the British Library.

Book designed and typeset by Bishan Samaddar, Seagull Books, Calcutta
Printed and bound by WordsWorth India, New Delhi, India

Contents

Answers

The following piece began life as a filmed interview with Jean Thibaudeau for the 'Archives du XXème siècle' (Archives of the Twentieth Century) series (1970). The film was first shown in full at the Centre Georges-Pompidou on the first anniversary of Barthes's death (26 March 1981).

Oeuvres complètes, Volume 3, pp. 1023–44

It was originally published in this edited form ten years earlier in Issue 47 (Autumn 1971) of the literary magazine *Tel Quel*, with which Barthes had a longstanding association. *Tel Quel* 47 was, in fact, a special number devoted to Barthes, containing articles on his work by Philippe Sollers, Julia Kristeva, François Wahl and Marc Buffat, together with a poem by Marcelin Pleynet and a text by Severo Sarduy, both prompted by aspects of his writing, and an article by Annette Lavers on the experience of translating Barthes into English. Thibaudeau who prepared the questions, was a member of *Tel Quel*'s editorial committee.

Barthes had published *S/Z* and *Empire of Signs* in 1970. In 1971, *Sade, Fourier, Loyola* would appear and this is presumably the 'recent text' to which he refers towards the end of the interview.

The footnotes to this interview are the translator's.

For a series of televised interviews, recorded under the general title 'Archives of the Twentieth Century'—though which will probably never be released, except perhaps on the death of the author—Jean Thibaudeau was kind enough to prepare for me a long, precise, direct and well-informed questionnaire relating (as was the rule) to both my life and work. This was, of course, a game by which neither he nor I could be taken in, coming as we did from a theoretical place where biography is held in low esteem. The interview took place, but it is possible to reproduce here only a small number of the very many questions that were asked. The answers have been re-written, but this does not mean that we are dealing here with writing [*écriture*], since, given the biographical intention, the 'I' (and its string of verbs in the past tense) must be embraced as though the person speaking were the same (were in the same place) as the person who lived. Consequently, we shall have to remind ourselves that the person who was born at the same time as I was, on 12 November 1915, is going to become continuously, by the mere effect of enunciation, an entirely 'imaginary' first person. In what follows, then, it will be necessary implicitly to re-establish the quotation marks that it is appropriate to put around any naively referential utterance. All biography is a novel that dares not speak its name. (R.B.)

First questions: birth, family, class origin, childhood . . .

I was born during the 14–18 war (at the end of 1915, on 12 November) at Cherbourg, a town I don't know, since I literally never set foot in it, having existed for only two months when I left. My father was a naval officer. He was killed in 1916 during a naval battle in the Strait of Dover; I was eleven months old.

The class I belong to is, I think, the bourgeoisie. So you may judge, I'll run through the list of my four grandparents (this is what the Vichy regime did under the Nazi occupation to determine the quantity of Jew-ishness in an individual). My paternal grandfather, an official of the Chemins de Fer du Midi railway com-pany, was descended from a line of notaries who lived in a small town in the Tarn département (Mazamet, I'm told). My paternal grandmother's parents were impoverished provincial nobles (from the Tarbes area). My maternal grandfather, Captain Binger, who came of an Alsatian family of master glaziers, was an explorer; in 1887–89 he explored the area south of the river Niger. As for my maternal grandmother, the only well-off member of that constellation, her parents came from Lorraine and had a small foundry in Paris. On my father's side the family was Catholic and on my mother's side, Protestant. As my father was dead, I was brought up in the—Calvinist—faith of my mother.

To sum up, there is in my social origins, one quarter of property-owning bourgeoisie, one quarter of ancient nobility and two quarters of liberal bourgeoisie, all of it mixed up and unified by a general impoverishment. That bourgeoisie was, in fact, either poor, sometimes to the point of seriously straitened circumstances, or lacking in generosity. This meant that when my mother became a 'war widow' and I a 'war orphan', my mother learnt a manual trade—bookbinding—and we lived with some difficulty from this in Paris, where we had moved when I was ten.

I regard the South-West as my 'homeland'—it's the country of my father's family, of my childhood and my adolescent holidays (I still go back often, though I no longer have relatives or friends there). Bayonne, where my paternal grandparents lived, is a town that played a Proustian role in my past—and a Balzacian one too, since that was where I listened, during my visits, to the talk of a certain provincial bourgeoisie, finding it, from a very early age, more entertaining than oppressive.

Other biographical questions: your adolescence, studies?

I spent my adolescence in Paris, always in the Saint-Germain-des-Prés area (a provincial quarter in those days): rue Jacob, rue Bonaparte, rue Mazarine, rue Jacques Callot, rue de Seine; I still live quite nearby.

But I always spent the three school holidays of the year at Bayonne at my grandmother's and aunt's, who lived in a house in the Allées Paulmy which had a large garden and had once been a rope factory. At Bayonne I read a great deal (such novels as I could find, most of which came from a reading room in the rue Gambetta) and, above all, I played a lot of music. My aunt was a piano teacher and I heard that instrument played there all day (even the scales didn't bore me) and, as soon as the piano was free, I myself sat down at it and picked my way through some music. I composed little pieces long before I could write. And later, before I fell ill, I took singing lessons with Charles Panzéra for whom I still have immense admiration and who has been so kind as not to have forgotten me. Even today, when I'm trying to clarify notions of literary theory apparently far removed from classical music and my youth, I sometimes reach back to something from Panzéra within me—not his philosophy, but his precepts, his way of singing, of pronouncing, of *taking* sounds, of annihilating psychological expressiveness beneath a purely musical production of pleasure. These are clarifications that are still present to me: if I want to know what (the French) language is, I have only to put on his record of Fauré's *Bonne Chanson*, though that is, sadly, a re-pressing. It was Panzéra's misfortune that he had to stop singing just before the advent of microgroove vinyl records, thus ceding a place which, for the current generation, has come to be unjustly filled by the indiscreet Fischer-Dieskau.

I was educated first at the *lycée* in Bayonne, then at the lycée Montaigne in Paris, finishing my secondary studies at the lycée Louis-le-Grand. Two months before the baccalaureate (philosophy option), on 10 May 1934, I coughed up blood and left for 'open-door' treatment in the Pyrenees—at Bedous in the Aspe valley. That incident put paid to my 'vocation'—until my illness, being 'good at arts subjects', I had planned to go to the École normale supérieure. But when I came back to Paris in 1935, I was happy just to read for a degree in classics—a meagre commitment,[1] which I made up for by founding the Sorbonne Ancient Theatre Group with a fellow student, Jacques Veil, who is no longer with us (he was murdered by the Nazis). I took an active part in the group (to the detriment of my academic grades) until about 1939.

What 'milieu' shaped you?

What is a 'milieu'? A language space, a network of connections, of supportive or exemplary figures. In that

[1] Students from the 'preparatory classes' of the prestigious *lycées*, such as Louis-le-Grand, normally aspired to enter one of the *grandes écoles* (such as the École normale supérieure), where they would prepare for France's highest academic examination, the *agrégation*. They would be simultaneously enrolled at a university, but studying for a degree would constitute only part of their studies.

ROLAND BARTHES

sense, I had no 'milieu'. I spent my adolescence alone with my mother, who was herself socially 'disconnected' (though not *déclassée*), perhaps quite simply because she worked. We didn't have any 'connections'. My only milieu was that of the grammar school and my only communication was with my classmates. The circle around my grandparents in Bayonne could no doubt be called a 'milieu', but I've already said that I saw that 'milieu' as a sort of show [*un spectacle*]. This doesn't mean that I wasn't shaped by a certain—bourgeois—style of life, despite our poverty (you may take my answer in the following way—the Mother is detached from the milieu; she is innocent of it and spared its little habits. She is, in and of herself a 'good' milieu, or she is, at least, what filters out the milieu. In a sense, then, she staves off social alienation). As for the cultural environment, it was essentially a written one, consisting of the books to be found in the home— some classics, some Anatole France, [Marcel] Proust, [André] Gide, [Paul] Valéry, the novels of the 20s and 30s. There was no Surrealism, philosophy or criticism and certainly no Marxism—we read *L'Oeuvre*, a radical-socialist, pacifist, anticlerical newspaper, a left-wing newspaper by the standards of the day.

What was your experience of the war like? Who were you, intellectually and politically, at the Liberation?

I went through more or less the whole of the war in a sanatorium bed. I'd been exempted from military service on account of my first bout of tuberculosis. When war was declared I was appointed to teach at the *lycée* in Biarritz (third and fourth forms). Then, coming back to Paris after France was defeated, I was a supervisor[2] at the lycée Voltaire and the lycée Carnot. I then suffered a relapse of my tuberculosis (in 1941) and went off for treatment at the Students' Sanatorium at Saint-Hilaire-du-Touvet in the Isère department. Then, after a brief return to Paris and a new relapse, I was treated at Leysin in Switzerland from 1943 to 46. It was a long period which was, more or less, that of the Occupation. In the sanatorium, except towards the end when I felt sick of the system, overwhelmed by it, I was happy—I read and I gave over a lot of time and energy to my friendships. At one point I considered abandoning my studies on the arts side to turn to medicine (I wanted to do psychiatry). I began studying for what was then called the PCB certificate,[3] but a minor relapse halted me and I was happy enough just to finish my classics degree (I had earned my Higher Studies Diploma before the end of my degree with a man I liked a great deal, the Hellenist Paul Mazon, on the subject of incantations and invocations in Greek tragedy). During my stay in the sanatorium, I wrote some articles for the establishment's student magazine,

---

2 The role of the *surveillant* or *pion* (Barthes uses the latter, more informal term) was largely to supervise students' private study.

3 A preliminary scientific qualification in physics, chemistry and biology.

ROLAND BARTHES

Existences—most notably on [Albert] Camus's *The Outsider* which had just been published—and in them I formed the first idea of 'white' writing or, in other words, the zero degree of writing.

At Leysin, at the university clinic where there were some thirty of us receiving treatment, a friend called [Georges] Fournié talked to me convincingly about Marxism. He was a former typesetter, a Trotskyite activist back from the camps.[4] The intelligence, suppleness and force of his political analyses, his irony and his wisdom, a sort of moral freedom—in a word, the total roundedness of this character, who seemed free of any political *excitability*—gave me a very elevated idea of the Marxist dialectic (or, more accurately, what I perceived in Marxism was—thanks to Fournié—the dialectic). I discovered the same seductiveness subsequently only when I read [Bertolt] Brecht. On the other hand, 1945–46 was the period when we were discovering [Jean-Paul] Sartre. At the Armistice, to answer your question as directly and briefly as possible, I was, then, a Sartrean and a Marxist. I was trying to make literary form *engagé* (I had a strong sense that this was the case with Camus's *Outsider*) and to Marxize Sartre's *engagement* or, at the least—and this was perhaps inadequate—to supply it with a Marxist justification. This is a twofold project that can be seen fairly clearly in *Writing Degree Zero*.

4 He was a survivor of Buchenwald.

How did you come to literary criticism?

Have I actually come to it? Or, at the very least, is it actually literary criticism that I've come to? I'll just describe some of the circumstances here. The friend I mentioned, Fournié, knew Maurice Nadeau, who was the editor of the literary page of *Combat* which, as you will remember, was very important at the time. I presented Nadeau with a short text (this must have been around 1946) on the idea of white writing and the commitment of form. Nadeau asked me for two articles for *Combat*. I gave him them (in 1947). This was the origin of *Writing Degree Zero*, since a little later, after a period as French lector at Bucharest and Alexandria, when I came back to Paris and became a (relatively free) bureaucrat in the General Directorate of Cultural Relations, I developed this theme in some new articles for *Combat* (in 1950). Apart from Nadeau, to whom I owe that crucial thing that is a beginning, two men showed an interest in these first texts and asked me to turn them into a book: Raymond Queneau (though Gallimard turned down the manuscript), and Albert Béguin who, with Jean Cayrol, took me on for Éditions du Seuil, by whom I'm still published.

Your first book, in 1953, was Writing Degree Zero. *That short work represents an exceptionally assured debut. Were you, subjectively, 'sure' of yourself (of your capabilities and your plans)?*

The 'subject' (we were not clearly aware of this at the time) is 'divided'. So, subjectively, I was too. As a subject involved in a struggle or what I regarded as such—namely, to demonstrate the political and historical engagement of literary language—I was sure of myself. But as a subject producing an object offered publicly for the gaze of others, I was rather shamefaced. I can remember one evening, after it became certain that *Writing Degree Zero* would be published by Éditions du Seuil, I was walking along the boulevard Saint-Michel and, all alone, I reddened up at the thought that the book could no longer be taken back again. This sense of panic still grips me today after having written certain texts (and I'm not even talking here about my reluctance—which is, all in all, a fear—to reread my past books). Suddenly the power of words seems exorbitant and the responsibility for them unbearable. I feel too weak before my own writing. And yet I go on. I release the text into circulation, because I tell myself that this is just an illusory moment in the work of writing, the—perhaps inevitable—phase in which you still believe that, like speech, it is an exposed part of your body and because of that sort of philosophy which has me believe that writing cannot avoid being terroristic (a terror that can turn around against its author) and that it's laughable to want to take it back again. At the very most, I correct those things in my text which seem to represent too great a risk of stupidity or aggressiveness—I let some of its features *drift*.

To what critical systems or theories of literature is Writing Degree Zero *indebted? Did [Jean] Paulhan, [Maurice] Blanchot or Sartre play a part in shaping you? And on the Marxist side, were you familiar, in particular, with [György] Lukács's work?*

I wasn't aware of any critical system or theory of literature ('system' and 'theory' weren't part of the vocabulary in those existentialist days). I didn't know Paulhan or Blanchot or Lukács. I suspect I wasn't even aware of their names (with the possible exception of Paulhan). I knew Marx, a little of Lenin, a little of Trotsky and all the Sartre it was possible to know at the time. And I'd read a lot of literature (in the sanatorium).

Do you want to give a justification for the writers 'excluded' from Writing Degree Zero *(for example, [Antonin] Artaud, [Georges] Bataille, [Francis] Ponge, etc.)?*

These 'exclusions' were instances of ignorance. I didn't know Artaud, Bataille or Ponge. You can, of course, transform this ignorance into 'exclusion'. But then you have to put that down to my unconscious or my laziness and I leave it to potential critics to do that sort of thing. In these problems of intellectual chronology, you seem to be improperly projecting the present into the past—to be unaware of Bataille in 1950 didn't have the same meaning as being unaware of him today. It was the same with Lukács. Who knew Lukács in the post-war years, except for [Henri] Lefebvre or [Lucien]

Goldmann? You seem to take the view that there's a sort of intellectual morality that obliges the essayist to be systematically curious about the production going on around him. I've always written with infinitely more opacity, infinitely less reading than you think. Injustice, partiality, chance and even a restricted choice of reading in no way prevent one from writing—and, if need be, writing about current matters.

Your life up until the Michelet book?

I stayed in the Education Service of the Cultural Relations directorate for two or three years. My work there was concerned with honorary doctorates and foreign trips for teachers at religious schools. In 1952, I got a grant from the CNRS to write a thesis in lexicology on the vocabulary of the social question in France around 1830. I should say that, during my time in Alexandria—in 1950—I had got to know [Algirdas Julien] Greimas who taught there as I did. Thanks to Greimas, I began to work on linguistics and, through him, I came to know [Georges] Matoré. So I became interested in lexicology or the sociology of lexica.

In 1954, you published Michelet par lui-même.[5] *Was that entirely your own choice? Or were there also external circumstances that gave rise to the book?*

5 Translated into English by Richard Howard simply as *Michelet* (New York: Hill & Wang, 1987).

When I was a student, I used to see a man called Joseph Baruzi, the brother of the religious historian Jean Baruzi who was a specialist on Saint John of the Cross. Joseph Baruzi was stimulating in many ways and had an extraordinary knowledge of cultural 'marginalia'— he knew how to draw the enigmatic aspects out of unfashionable material. It was he who got me reading [Jules] Michelet and I was immediately impressed by certain pages (particularly, as I recall, on the egg)—no doubt on account of their baroque force. Subsequently, at Leysin (the Swiss universities lent out their books to tuberculosis patients, whereas, for fear of contagion, the French did not), I was able to read the whole of Michelet. I copied the phrases or sentences which appealed to me, for whatever reason, on to record cards—or simply those that occurred more than once. As I arranged those record cards, rather as you might play with a pack of playing cards, I arrived inevitably at a thematics. When the Éditions du Seuil (in the person of Francis Jeanson, I think) asked me to produce a book in their 'Écrivains de toujours' series, it only remained to write it up. That thematic analysis owed nothing to [Gaston] Bachelard, for the very good reason that I hadn't read him. However, that never seemed a sufficient reason to protest every time someone connected the Michelet book with Bachelard— why would I *reject* association with Bachelard?

Will you tell us something about your participation in Théâtre populaire?

There were two periods to *Théâtre populaire*. In the first, we ([Robert] Voisin, [Bernard] Dort, [Guy] Dumur, [Jean] Duvignaud, [Jean] Paris, Morvan Lebesque and I) endeavoured to defend—and even to produce criticism of—[Jean] Vilar's Théâtre national populaire, given that it was, all things considered, good popular theatre. Vilar was trying to break down the institution of the bourgeois audience while retaining, in his conception of the drama, a demand for aesthetic refinement. But he didn't have—or didn't want to have—any ideological culture. So the second period of *Théâtre populaire* began when Brecht and the Berliner Ensemble came to France (in 1954). The radical campaign we fought at that time, at our particular level—particularly, Voisin, Dort and I—in favour of Brecht, of Brechtian theory and dramaturgy, made us a lot of enemies. Some people left us; others spent their time either disputing the existence of the *difference* we saw in Brechtian theatre or ironizing on the supposed intellectualism of Brechtian concepts (alienation effect, 'social *Gestus*', 'epic' theatre, etc.)—we don't like to mix intellect and art in France—or, alternatively, protesting against the 'dogmatism' and 'terrorism' of French Brechtianism.

You've always maintained this reference to Brecht (as, for example, in 'Literature and Signification' of 1963[6]).

6 The English translation of this text is published in Barthes's *Critical Essays* (Richard Howard trans.) (Evanston, IL: Northwestern University Press, 2000), pp. 261–79.

Why? Does Brecht's exemplary status have to do with the Marxist foundations of his work?

I've written on two occasions (albeit at no great length) about the impact Brechtian theatre had on me and the reasons why, once I'd acquired a sense of that form of theatre, it was difficult for me to like—or even watch—another kind. Moreover, I'm possibly going to write seriously on Brecht again in the near future. Brecht is still a very topical question for me, all the more so, perhaps, as he isn't fashionable and he still hasn't made it into the axiomatic field of the avant-garde. His exemplarity, as I see it, has to do neither, strictly speaking, with his Marxism or with his aesthetic (though each of these is tremendously important) but with the combination of the two—the combination of Marxist reasoning and a thinking on semantics. He was a Marxist who had thought about *the effects of signs*, which is a rarity.

You haven't published a book on theatre. Your writings on the theatre are either scattered across Mythologies, On Racine *and* Critical Essays *or haven't been republished in book form. Why is this?*

Simply because no one's asked me.

Mythologies *appears in 1957. We're talking here initially about a set of short texts published between 1954 and 1956, mainly in the literary magazine* Les Lettres nouvelles. *A first question: What does a magazine mean to you so far as your work, your 'writing' is concerned?*

One of the first effects of writing (whether you're fearful of it or welcome it) is that you don't know *who you're talking to—writing* isn't transferential (which is why many 'orthodox' psychoanalysts reject the idea of a psychoanalytic literary criticism). In the work of writing, the literary magazine represents a kind of intermediate stage between speech, which involves a precise *ad hominem* address and the book, which involves none at all. When you write a text for a magazine, you're not so much thinking of the readership of the magazine (in any case, the readership is scarcely 'thinkable') but its group of editors. They have the advantage of forming a sort of collective—but not, strictly speaking, public—addressee. It's like a workshop or a 'class' (the way one speaks of the 'violin class' at a music school)—you write for the 'class'. The magazine—all tactical considerations of solidarity and struggle apart; I'm not talking about those here—is a stage in writing. It's the stage at which you write to be liked by those you know, the cautious, reasonable stage, where you *begin* to relax—without yet breaking—the transferential umbilical cord of language (you never entirely put this stage behind you: If I didn't have friends and if I didn't have to write for them, would I still have the heart to write? You're always coming back to magazines).

In the '57 preface, you present Mythologies *as an attempt to 'track down . . . the ideological abuse' within 'the decorative display of what-goes-without-saying.' Can you tell us more precisely what your political position was in the '50s?*

The aim of *Mythologies* isn't political but ideological (paradoxically, in our age and our France, there seem to be more ideological twists and turns than political ones). What *Mythologies* does is take on *wholesale* and systematically a kind of monster I've called the 'petty bourgeoisie' (at the risk of making a myth out of it) and keep hammering away at it. The method isn't at all scientific and made no pretensions to being so. This is why the attempt at a methodology only came afterwards, through a reading of Saussure. The theory of *Mythologies* is dealt with in a 'postface'. And it's a partial theory only, since, though a *semiological* version of ideology was sketched out there, it needed—and still needs—to be complemented by a political theory of the petty-bourgeois phenomenon. Since I'm still in the process of settling accounts with the petty bourgeoisie (more, no doubt, than with the bourgeoisie), I sometimes have in mind if not to write a big book, then at least to undertake a big project on the petty bourgeoisie, during which I'd learn from others (political theorists, economists and sociologists) what it is politically and economically, and how to define it in terms of criteria that aren't purely cultural. My (highly ambivalent) interest in the petty bourgeoisie derives, in fact, from the following assumption (or working hypothesis)—that culture today is barely 'bourgeois' any longer, but 'petty bourgeois'. Or, at least, that the petty bourgeoisie is currently trying to elaborate its own culture by *debasing* bourgeois culture. Bourgeois culture is making its historical comeback, but this time as *farce* (you'll remember the schema Marx alludes to).[7] That 'farce' is so-called mass culture.

You've several times stressed the importance in your 'development' of the essay 'Myth Today' (1956) that closes Mythologies. *After* Mythologies, *you went five years without publishing another book. Although your later works include texts that were written in those years, does this silence indicate a 'crisis'? Or 'difficulties' of a 'poetic' or scientific order?*

The years 1956–63 were, in some ways, a time of professional instability. As I said, I'd begun a thesis in lexicology, but I soon ran up against methodological difficulties I was unable to resolve. At the time, I didn't even suspect that they were 'interesting' (let's say, for simplicity's sake, that these concerned the difficulty of classifying not words, which lexicology was more than able to do, but syntagms, stereotypes—for example, 'commerce and industry'—which was to pose the problem of what might be termed associative semantics). I wasn't getting anywhere and my CNRS grant

7 'Hegel remarks somewhere that all great world-historic facts and personages appear, so to speak, twice. He forgot to add: the first time as tragedy, the second time as farce.' Karl Marx, 'The Eighteenth Brumaire of Louis Bonaparte', *Surveys from Exile* (David Fernbach ed., Ben Fowkes trans.) (Harmondsworth: Penguin Books, 1973), p. 146.

was withdrawn. Robert Voisin helped me at that point, taking me to the Éditions de l'Arche with him. Then, thanks to support from Lucien Febvre and Georges Friedmann, I came back to the CNRS, but this time in sociology. I began work on a sociology—or, more exactly, a socio-semiology—of clothing, which led subsequently to *The Fashion System*. Some years later (I don't recall the date), I lost my CNRS grant a second time but, fortunately, I was picked up once again, this time by Fernand Braudel, who took me to the École pratique des hautes études as a *chef de travaux*. I became a director of studies there in 1962, offering a seminar on 'The Sociology of Signs, Symbols and Representations'. That was a compromise title—what I wanted to do was semiology (hence 'signs' and 'symbols'), but I didn't want to cut myself off from sociology (hence 'collective representations', an expression from Durkheimian sociology).

Intellectually, I don't think there was a 'crisis' in that period. Quite the contrary. And I don't really know if it's a 'crisis' that stops one producing books or the opposite—confidence, drive and an enthusiasm for acquiring and conveying information. For me, it was more the latter. With Saussure having enabled me (at least as I believed) to define ideology by way of the semantic schema of connotation, I fervently believed it possible to become part of a semiological *science*. I went through a time of dreaming (euphorically) of scientificity (*The Fashion System* and *Elements of*

Semiology are the residues of that dream). It wasn't so important to me, then, to write books. There was time for that later. And indeed, as you've noted, I was writing a lot of articles, which kept up my writing (my desire to write). What has happened since—at least up to the present—has shown that the second aspiration is where my 'truth' lies, not the first, though I do still often have to support that aspiration as a 'semiologist', a status which some confirm and others contest.

Two of your books have a proper name in the title. Are Michelet and Racine particularly important writers for you, as emblematic of nineteenth-century and classical literature respectively or do you see them as significant in themselves? And are they 'favourite' writers of yours? What is a 'favourite' writer? And who are 'your' favourite writers?

I've talked about the personal origin of the *Michelet*. *Racine* was simply a commissioned work. [Claude] Grégory of the Club français du livre publishing house asked me to write a preface for Chateaubriand's *Memoirs*. I was very happy to do that, but the professor who'd established the 'correct' text wouldn't let Grégory have it and he, needing a book on Racine, asked me to write one ('A calculator was needed, it was a dancer that got it'[8]). I happen to dislike Racine as much as I

---

8 Pierre de Beaumarchais, *The Marriage of Figaro* (1784), Act V, Scene 3.

like Michelet. I only managed to interest myself in him by forcing myself to inject personal problems of alienation in love. As for a 'favourite' author, I think that's simply someone you reread periodically. In that case—and staying with the classics—my particularly 'favourite' authors are Sade, Flaubert and Proust.

Which works of linguistics or from other scientific disciplines have shaped your semiological research?

It's a whole culture, the infinite set of things read and conversations, albeit sometimes hastily gleaned and poorly digested snippets (in short, the intertext), that presses upon a piece of work and seeks admittance to it. To quote names, I'd say in my case that the semiological urge comes from Saussure, whom I read in 1956 (though I'd read a 'minor' structuralist, Viggo Brøndal, as early as 1947, taking the 'zero degree' notion from him). I owe a great deal, as I've said, to the conversations I had with Greimas from 1950 onwards; he introduced me very early on to [Roman] Jakobson's theory of shifters and to the formal significance of certain figures like metaphor, metonymy, catalysis and ellipsis. [Louis] Hjelmslev enabled me to develop and formalize the schema of connotation, a notion that's always been very important to me and one I can't do without, though there's a risk of presenting denotation as a natural state of language and connotation as a cultural state. I have to say that it's only now, with a considerable delay, that I've turned my attention to [Noam] Chomsky. I read [Vladimir] Propp in English, though I don't remember precisely when, after a conversation with [Claude] Lévi-Strauss, and [Victor] Erlich's book on the Russian Formalists too, before [Tzvetan] Todorov's anthology came out. But of all the linguists I've read, [Émile] Benveniste remains the most eminent for me, a writer so shamefully forgotten and abandoned today. There is on the surface of his linguistics something like a simmering (poignant, because so understated) of water that's about to boil; that force, that warmth that raises science (the most rigorous science that there is, in Benveniste's case) towards *something else* is, as you know, what I call 'writing'. We are coming here to very contemporary matters (Lévi-Strauss, [Jacques] Lacan, Todorov, [Gérard] Genette, [Jacques] Derrida, [Julia] Kristeva, *Tel Quel*, [Philippe] Sollers) which will be the subject of the seminar I want to work on for 1971–72. For though it was, indeed, linguistics that provided the operational framework for semiology, this has been modified and taken further in the light of other disciplines, other forms of thinking, other exigencies—ethnology, philosophy, Marxism, psychoanalysis, the theory of writing and the text (though it must also be said that it's wrong to bring all these disciplines under the heading of semiology just because one's a 'semiologist': there is here a general dislocation towards *something else*).

In 1965, a short book by Professor Raymond Picard entitled Nouvelle Critique ou nouvelle imposture? *rounded violently on the new French criticism—and on you in particular. That attack received 'uncritical, total and unreserved support' from a large section of the press.[9] What hostilities have you aroused since 1953? Did this Picard Affair have antecedents? Were you expecting it?*

I'll reply with reference more to the future than the past, since, though the Picard Affair is over, nothing *precludes it from recurring*. By this I mean that on the historic stage of the Signifier, it may return. I shall even venture to say that, in a relatively static society, by mere effect of the repetition compulsion, it *must* return. The actors will be new but the *site* will be the same. I've always been struck by the fact that Picard's arguments—or, rather, his turns of phrase—though they apparently arise out of an over-aestheticizing view of literature, could very well have come from—and hence can very well come in future—from a contrary place: historicism, positivism or sociologism, for example. This is because these places are actually just one site, which is, roughly speaking, that of *asymbolia*; on the other side of psychoanalysis, there is just one single place, and its occupants (the actors) may change but not its topological function. Though I by no means

---

9 Roland Barthes, *Criticism and Truth* (Katrine Pilcher Tody trans.) (London: Continuum, 2007), p. 18, note 2.

wish it, I shouldn't be surprised if, one day, a certain kind of university supplants the traditional one and Picard is reborn as some positivistic, sociologistic or 'Marxist' censor (I use inverted commas here to indicate that this would be a *particular* kind of Marxism). Such people already exist.

The Fashion System *was published in 1967. You present the book as 'a kind of slightly naive stained-glass window' in which the reader should find, 'not the certainties of a doctrine, nor even the unvarying conclusions of an investigation, but rather the beliefs, the temptations and the trials of an apprenticeship'.*[10] *Why is there still this naivety in 1967—ten years after* Mythologies? *Is your work condemned to be always at the 'trial stages' of a learning process that will never end?*

I had in mind initially to develop a serious socio-semiology of clothing, of all clothing (I'd even begun some practical research), but then, as a result of a private comment made to me by Lévi-Strauss, I decided to homogenize the corpus and confine myself to *written* clothing—i.e. clothing described by the fashion magazines. Because of this change, *The Fashion System* came out a long time after it had been conceived and even a long time after most of the work had

10 Roland Barthes, *The Fashion System* (Matthew Ward and Richard Howard trans) (Berkeley: University of California Press, 1990), pp. *ix–x*. Translation modified.

been done. In those years, intellectual history was advancing very quickly. The unfinished manuscript was getting to seem dated and I even hesitated over publishing it. And perhaps, too, I wasn't expecting anything—any pleasure, shall we say—from the book's publication; the whole delight of it lay in elaborating and developing the system, working on that long and passionately, rather as you might work on solving a problem in physics or knocking up some complicated but useless object. There was scant pleasure to be had from laying out the findings, which can be detected in the way it's drafted (this proves yet again that the *imaginary* of science exempts its practitioners from writing, but also gets it wrong—and thereby gets the truth wrong). *The Fashion System* was in thrall to scientificity. I believed at the time that, once the semiological theory was established, then particular semiotics had to be constructed, semiotics *applied* to pre-existing sets of cultural objects—food, clothing, narratives, cities, etc. It's this deductive view which subsequently seemed to me rather 'naive'. The 'common sense' that seems to dictate such an approach is, in fact, the product of the scientist's *imaginary* (I use this term in the Lacanian sense). In other words, what was naive was to believe in meta-language.

On the infinite character of learning I'll say this—it isn't learning that never ends but desire. My work seems to be the product of a series of 'disinvestments'; there's only one object from which I have never disinvested my desire and that is language. Language is *my object little-a*. From *Writing Degree Zero* onwards (and probably since adolescence, when I perceived the discourse of the provincial bourgeoisie as spectacle), it's language I've chosen to love—and, of course, to hate at the same time, being both entirely trusting and thoroughly distrustful towards it. But my methods of approaching it, dependent on findings being arrived at around me, which exerted their particular fascinations, may have changed. At times I was simply trying my hand, seeking to please, working to change myself or giving myself up to a particular language—it's as though one was still loving the same person but experimenting with new forms of eroticism. *The endless learning process* shouldn't be understood here as part of some humanist programme, as though one ought always to be dissatisfied with oneself and to be progressing ('maturing') towards some Olympian image fashioned out of knowledge and wisdom, but, rather, as the inevitable course of what Lacan calls 'the revolutions of desire'.

In 1970, if we bear in mind the anxieties of many teachers, particularly in 'the arts and human sciences', the dedication in S/Z *looks rather provocative: 'This book is the trace of work done during a two-year seminar (1968–69) at the École pratique des hautes études. I hope that the students, auditors, and friends who took part in this seminar will accept this dedication of a text which was written according to their attention* [écoute] *to it.' Don't you think these lines may irritate some teachers whose teaching is being contested?*

It's my firm belief that, between them, students and teachers very often arrive at ways of working communally; at any rate, that's the normal way of things at the École pratique des hautes études. If the dedication you refer to contains a paradox, it isn't the one you mention but a different one which hasn't generally been noticed. Some have thought that *S/Z* came out of *discussions* between the students and the director of studies. They didn't see that the dedication (above and beyond its genuinely friendly character) was crafted to introduce the word *écoute*.[11] The paradox, with regard to both academic discourse and the discourse of protest, lies in the implication that it makes no sense to me to present the 'lecture' form as being in opposition to a class in which there is 'dialogue'. Liberation doesn't consist in giving the student the right to speak (a minimal measure) but in trying to modify the circuit of speech—not its physical circuit (one party speaking rather than the other), but its topological circuit (I'm referring here to psychoanalysis, of course). In other words, it consists in becoming aware of the true dialectic (in the Lacanian, not Platonic, sense) of the teaching relationship. By the terms of that dialectic, listening isn't simply active—which doesn't actually mean much— *listening is productive*. By echoing back to me, albeit silently, though by their renewed presence, the analysis

11 Translated here as attention, but more literally 'listening'.

ROLAND BARTHES

of *Sarrasine* that I was carrying out, the audience, to whom I was bound by a transferential relationship, were constantly modifying my own discourse.

On the other hand, why devote two years to a short story by Balzac when, as you yourself have stated, the 'requirement for ideological criticism' has 'suddenly re-emerged'?

I'll reply first as follows, following on from what I've just said about 'listening'. Two years may seem quite a long time to 'explicate' a few pages of Balzac but may perhaps represent a good length for a period of transference. What basically distinguishes a seminar from a lecture—and why I like seminars and don't like lectures—is that in the former case a dialectic can develop, whereas in the latter we're simply dealing with a linguistic show of force. *Because it lasts*—and does so in relation to a single object—a seminar has many 'adventures' going on beneath the surface (I'm referring, as ever, to adventures of the signifier). As I see it, the object of a seminar doesn't lie chiefly in its syllabus ('producing a textual analysis of a Balzac short story') but in the knowledge of language that's being sought and exercised tacitly.

As for ideological criticism, that's the pet theme of the new University. Everyone's agreed on that. The difficulty begins when you try to decide where ideology lies, or, rather, *whether there is a place from which ideology is absent* (that place isn't necessarily the one from which the critic of ideologies speaks). I don't think ideology stops *short of* Balzac (in relation to us) or, rather (since my object of study wasn't Balzac but the text), *short of* the classical narrative. It's precisely because the demand for ideological criticism has been made 'brutally evident' again in the last three years, as I said in the new preface to *Mythologies*,[12] that we should resist the temptation to offer a brute response to it by issuing declarations *on* ideology. The greater the demand, the more subtle should the response be; otherwise it would run the risk of being merely opportunistic or, at the very least, of being a mere sending of signals—one would be parading oneself as external to ideology without *first* asking oneself where ideology lies, and doesn't lie.

Starting out from Julia Kristeva's concept of intertextuality, how are we to distinguish the 'author of fiction' from the 'critic'? Or, alternatively, can S/Z be read as a 'rewriting' of Balzac?

The notion of intertext has, initially, a polemical significance—it serves to combat the law of *context*. Let me explain. Everyone knows that the context of a

---

12 '[I]deological criticism, at the very moment when the need for it was again made brutally evident (May '68), has become more sophisticated . . .' Roland Barthes, 'Preface to the 1970 Edition', *Mythologies* (Annette Lavers trans.) (St Albans: Paladin, 1976), p. 9.

ROLAND BARTHES

message (its material setting) reduces its polysemy. If you use the French word *jumelles*, which has two distinct meanings, it will be up to the rest of the sentence to eliminate one of the possible senses of the word and point definitely either to the signified 'binoculars' or '(female) twins'. In other words, the context reduces signification—or, to put it both more broadly and more precisely, *signifiance*—back to communication. To 'take account' of the context (in philology, in criticism, in linguistics) is always a *positive*, reductive, legalistic move, aligned to the clear precepts of rationalism. The context is, all in all, an asymbolic object. Take anyone who invokes context and, if you push a little, you'll always find a resistance to symbols, an asymbolia. The intertext (which, it must be repeated, is not at all the 'bench' of 'influences', 'sources' and 'origins' before which a work or an author might be summoned to appear) is, much more widely and at a quite other level, that field where what Sollers has (in his article on Dante) magnificently and indelibly termed the *traversal of writing* takes place; it is the text *in its traversing and its being traversed* (in this equivalence between active and passive you'll recognize the particular way the unconscious works). Among other things, this means that the intertext recognizes no division of genres; all questions of value aside, the commentary of *S/Z* is regarded as being *on an equal footing* with Balzac's text (like two stretches of a canal brought to the same level by the operation of a lock).

It isn't wrong, then, to say that *S/Z* is a rewriting of *Sarrasine*—on condition that we add immediately that it isn't 'I' who wrote *S/Z*, but 'we'—all those I tacitly or unconsciously cited or called on and which are 'readings' [*des 'lectures'*], not 'authors'.

As for the more precise opposition between fiction and criticism, I've often had occasion to say that this was being abolished in the current crisis of the novel, in the crisis of criticism and with the coming of the Text. Let's say that, in the transitional state of current production, the roles are simply scrambled without yet being abolished. For my part, I don't regard myself as a critic but, rather, as a novelist or a scriptor—not of novels, admittedly, but of the 'novelistic'. *Mythologies* and *Empire of Signs* are novels *without* a story; *On Racine* and *S/Z* are novels *about* stories; *Michelet* is a para-biography, etc. This is why I might say that my own historical position (there is always room for self-questioning on this) is to be in the rearguard of the avant-garde. Being avant-garde means knowing what is dead; being 'rearguard' means still loving it—I love the novelistic but I know the novel is dead. There we have, I think, the exact place from which I write.

Certain pages in Empire of Signs *are reminiscent of the 'realism' of the texts in* Mythologies—*the former utopian, the latter, in 1957, satirical. Picking up on the formula you applied to Voltaire, we might be tempted to say that you are, very paradoxically, since the questioning of literature is crucial to you, 'the last happy writer'.*[13]

What do you owe to the eighteenth century (to Voltaire, Montesquieu, Diderot, etc.)?

The little tableaux of *Empire of Signs* are happy Mythologies, perhaps because, leaving aside certain personal reasons, my artificial situation as a tourist in Japan—though a lost tourist, in short, an ethnographer—enabled me to 'forget' the Japanese petty bourgeoisie, the impact it surely exerts on manners, the art of living and the style of objects, etc. I was spared the sickening effect of mythology. One of my hypothetical projects is, precisely, to *forget* (by what would be a far greater effort) the French petty bourgeoisie, and to catalogue the few 'pleasures' still available to me living in France. If it were ever to see the light of day, I could call that book *Our France*, in reference to Michelet, who left us an apocryphal work of that name.[14] It will, of course, require a dialectical labour, since I'll never be able to abstract present-day France from its political history, as I did with Japan. Moreover, since I'm French, I'll have, as it were, to 'psychoanalyse myself', to know what it is in my origins that I'm abolishing, accepting and transforming.

13 The title of an article by Barthes on Voltaire, republished in his *Critical Essays*, pp. 83–9.

14 *Notre France*, nominally by Michelet, was actually a book compiled from his writings by his widow.

As for the eighteenth century, I've had no inclination until now to read its authors, which means that they're still there to be read—a pleasure I've very deliberately *kept in store for myself*, particularly where Diderot is concerned. The reason for this may seem artificial or flippant but I believe it chimes with the logic of my desire: a text touches me directly—ultimately, as it were[15]—through its language. Now, as I see it, the language of the eighteenth century (with the exception of Sade's, for reasons I've tried to lay out in a recent text) isn't marked. I can't see its code, its codes (which is no doubt the reason why it's described as 'elegant'). It's at this moment in history that class language becomes *natural*. So there's a kind of topsy-turviness here—the language I relish isn't the language of the progressive age (the language of the bourgeoisie already fully in possession of intellectual power), but the language of authoritarian times, the tangled, coded—and, so to speak, *flexed*—language (with its vast rhetorical structures) of the intellectually rising bourgeoisie, the prose of the seventeenth century. I have (regrettably, no doubt) read more [Jacques-Bénigne] Bossuet than [Denis] Diderot.

In Empire of Signs, *you write*: '*Writing is after all, in its way a* satori: satori (*the Zen occurrence*) *is a more or*

---

15 The French here, in both *Oeuvres complètes* and *Tel Quel 47* (Autumn 1971), is 'un texte m'atteint directement, d'une façon en quelque sorte ultime, par sa langue.'

ROLAND BARTHES

less powerful (though in no way solemn) seism which causes knowledge, or the subject, to vacillate: it creates a space devoid of speech. And it is also a space devoid of speech that constitutes writing.' [16] *What is this 'writing' by comparison with that of* Writing Degree Zero?

From writing as referred to in *Writing Degree Zero* to writing as we understand it today, there has been a slide in meaning and, so to speak, an inversion of terms. In *Writing Degree Zero*, writing is more of a sociological or, at any rate, socio-linguistic notion—it's the idiolect of a collectivity, an intellectual grouping and hence a sociolect situated at an intermediate point on the scale of communities between language, the system of a whole nation, and style, the system of a single subject. These days, I would prefer to call that sort of writing *écrivance* (in reference to the opposition between *écrivains* and *écrivants*), since writing (in the current sense) is, precisely, absent from it. And writing, in the new theory, would rather occupy the place of what I called style. In its traditional sense, style refers to matrices of utterances. I had attempted in 1947 to existentialize the notion, to 'give it flesh'. Today we go much further—'writing' isn't a personal idiolect (in the way that the old 'style' was); it is an uttering (not an utterance) through which the subject plays out its

---

16 Roland Barthes, *Empire of Signs* (Richard Howard, trans.) (New York: Hill and Wang, 1983), p. 4.

dividedness by dispersing itself, scattering itself all across that stage that is the blank page. Hence it's a notion that owes little to the old 'style' but a great deal, as you know, to a twofold illumination by materialism (the idea of productivity) and psychoanalysis (the idea of the divided subject).

What determines your programme of work? Do you always have work 'ahead of you'?

I only ever wrote one text 'for nothing'. That was my first text, the one I showed to Nadeau around 1946, which wasn't published but determined the requests that followed. Apart from that first 'zero' text, all the others have been written in response to requests (when I was left free to choose my subject) or commissions (when I was given a subject, which isn't something I necessarily dislike). All in all, I've always written in response to someone's prompting. Which means that, as life goes on and brings with it a growing number of relationships and situations, I have more and more work 'ahead of me'—and hence I'm always behind with things. I spend my life drawing up 'plans' for myself (in the hope that putting a project in my schedule will see it magically accomplished), which I pin up above my desk but then have to modify because they're already out of date. In the intellectual 'profession' (because it is a profession), there's a well-known sense of vertigo that arises from the contradiction between the pressure of the requests that come to you, which produce an illusion of vitality, as though you were someone *necessary*, and the non-necessary character [*gratuité*] of the practice of writing, which one uses as a rampart for oneself, as Lacan would say, by constantly telling oneself that it's a political, counter-ideological task, etc.—a labour required of us by history. One way of limiting this dizzying whirl, without going into the imaginary realm of false reasons, is, if I may put it this way, to treat writing as a proper job—that is to say, to make it a regular practice with strict hours. Personally, *come what may*, I try to set every morning aside for writing work.

Writing in response to a request (or a commission) is a 'job'. So I go from job to job, though that doesn't in any way exclude finding bliss in writing, nor even, if I may put it this way, the 'dreams' associated with it. A dream of writing isn't necessarily something compact. The plan to write a book isn't something you develop in an organized, deliberate, fully justified way. It comes from snatches of desire, fragments of longing that suddenly well up at any point of contact offered by life and don't necessarily relate to important ideas. Before a book's conceived, before you have the slightest idea what it will be—or even that it might exist one day—you can dream up an entirely final detail of that book, a particular fragment of a sentence *for which* you will produce the book or a particular typographical layout that you *see* (I believe a text can turn out *happily*—in other words, beyond the grasp of any sort of 'duty'—only if you can *see*, or I'd almost say, *hallucinate* the—written—typographical object into which it will transform itself). Lately, I've often dreamt of doing two things. On the one hand, writing a 'free' text that's wholly independent of any request or demand (however far back the origin of that might go), and hence a text that's open to formal experimentation (it's never a *form* that you're asked for—we're no longer living in the days when someone would ask you for a 'sonnet'), these experiments being conducted *at my own level and within my own limitations* and not based on models that originate necessarily with the avant-garde. On the other hand, devoting myself to acquiring a new skill, such as learning a language or a science or merely getting to know a subject very well—'thoroughly'. To do that, however, I'd have to find an object that wasn't too irrelevant or trivial (that wasn't a mere hobby and akin to stamp collecting), nor too close to current language and hence that didn't force me *too quickly* to perceive its modernity or significance. These dreams aren't unachievable. What stands in the way of them is more the ultimate awareness that they depend on an 'imaginary' and that the 'truth' of my work lies more at the point where a relatively precise *demand*, originating in the community *as it is* (a *commission*, if you like), introduces into my writing programme, immediately and, so to speak, naively—without intermediaries, excuses or transcendence—the desire of the Other. This is the condition on which—no doubt taking into account my own neurotic structure—I can *stay with* the signifier and not be disappointed too soon by its perpetual bounding away: it's within this very short *period of grace* that I write.

What is this interview that's coming to an end? What is the 'posterity' for which, in televisual form, it's apparently destined?

I'd like to take advantage of your question to put the idea of the interview in the dock. Not this particular interview, because it's biographical in its intentions and hence acceptable. Is it not, in fact, the only way to take on board what writing cannot—it is simply beyond it!—namely, the first person of the simple past? And I'm not talking about written interviews, question-naires where the response is entirely *generated* by writing. I'm talking about the usual kind of interview, the one that's spoken, recorded and then written up or, if you prefer the word, transcribed (but not 'written'). That sort of interview is very much in vogue today and there are no doubt economic (if not directly financial) grounds for that—the interview is an article on the cheap. 'You don't have time to write a piece for us? Well, grant us an interview then.' The old antinomy between thought and form resurfaces here—or, rather, their economy, their fallacious complicity (two old cronies). *Thought* is reputed to be immediate; it's assumed that no preparation is needed; it costs nothing and can be dispensed *directly*—the interview. Form, by contrast, has to be worked at; time is needed and effort; it costs a great deal—the article. Thought, it is suggested, doesn't need correcting, whereas style does. This is a thoroughly bourgeois view, and literally so, since the law of the bourgeois state (it dates from the Revolution) protects ownership of forms but not of ideas. This is a curious trick—thought is devalued and anonymized, while in the interviews it is sought and framed as something *personal*. This is because the mechanics of this practice are entirely theatrical—the interview is the emphatic sign of the fact that the author *thinks*: the spoken word is taken to be thought in the pure state; to note it down (without writing it) sanctions it as a responsible, consequential act: I am going to commit your thought to paper, therefore you are thinking. In the interview, the author *acts as if* he is thinking (I am questioning an institution here, not particular performances; I don't deny that some interviews are well thought out and, in some circumstances, useful; and, moreover, to systematically turn down interviews would be to fall into another role—of the secretive, untamed, anti-social thinker). In relation to writing (which isn't mere style), the interview seems even more pointless—if not, indeed, absurd. The supposition, in carrying it out, would seem to be that, having *written* something (a text or a book), the writer still has something to say. But what? Things they'd 'forgotten' or 'discarded'? Unless (as is commonly done) they're asked to repeat themselves or, which is worse, to say 'clearly' what they wrote 'densely' (but the ambiguity of meaning—or meanings— ellipsis, ambivalence, rhetorical figures, wordplay and anagrams that constitute writing aren't stylistic elements but an enunciatory practice that commits the subject in his/her wranglings with language). Writing is precisely what exceeds the spoken word; it is a supplement in which there isn't another Unconscious inscribed (there aren't two of them) but another relation of the speaker (or the listener) to the Unconscious. Hence speech cannot add anything to writing. What I have written about is *something I cannot now speak about*: What more would I say and what would I say better? One has to face the fact that speech always *lags behind* writing (and hence behind 'private life', which is simply an unfurling of speech: I am always, by necessity, more stupid, more naive, etc., than what I write). The only kind of interview one might at a pinch defend would be one in which the author were called upon to state what *he cannot* write. The good interviewer would then be someone who, abandoning the idea of representing the usual subjects of his books to the author, would have a reflective knowledge of *what belongs to speech and what to writing*, and would quiz the interviewee on what writing itself forbids him from writing. What writing never writes is 'I'. What speech always says is 'I'. What the interviewer should tease out is, therefore, the author's *imaginary*, his stock of phantasms, insofar as he can think them and speak them in that fragile state (which would be specifically the state of *interviewed speech*) in which they are sufficiently articulated to be spoken and not sufficiently liquidated to be able to be written (where I am concerned, for example, this would include music, food, travel, sexuality and work habits).

As for posterity, what am I to say? It's a dead word for me (which is only to repay it in kind, since it's something that acquires validity only with my death). I take the view that I've lived very well up to now (I mean happily, entertainingly, in a state of enjoyment) *with a small portion of my age and my country*. My life is entirely taken up in this simultaneity, this concomitance; I'm simply a *particular contemporary*, which means someone doomed, while I live, to exclusion from a great number of languages and, then, to absolute death. Buried away in the Archives (of the twentieth century), I'll perhaps emerge fleetingly from them one day as one speaker among others in an educational broadcast on 'structuralism', 'semiology' or 'literary criticism'. Can you imagine someone living, working and desiring just for that! Anyway, the only eschatological ideas I'm capable of can't be said to concern 'my' survival. If, one day, relations between subjects and the world change, some words will fall out of use, as in that Melanesian tribe where, with each death, they take a few elements out of the lexicon as a sign of mourning. Only, in this case, they'll be signs of joy. Or they'll at least be put in that museum of burlesque, social archaeology that Fourier dreamt of for the entertainment of the children of the phalanstery—this is, no doubt, what will happen to the word 'posterity' and perhaps even to all the 'possessives' in our language and—why not?—to the word 'death' itself. Can we not conceive of the creation of a community of such a kind (unprecedented for religions themselves) that the horrible solitude of death (experienced first in the fear of losing those one loves) would be impossible there? Won't there one day be a *socialist* solution to the horror of death? I can't see why death wouldn't be a socialist problem. Someone ([Georges] Gurvitch, I think) once quoted this quip by Lenin or Trotsky (I don't remember which, though it was in the middle of the October Revolution and the distinction didn't mean anything at that point): 'And if the sun is bourgeois, we'll stop the sun.' That's a specifically revolutionary saying (such as can only be produced in a revolutionary period). What Marxist today would dare to proclaim: 'And if death is bourgeois, we'll stop death'?

In your article on Kristeva's Sèméiotikè *('L'étrangère', 1970), you write that, 'in a society deprived of any socialist practice and hence condemned to "discourse", theoretical discourse is provisionally necessary'. Do you mean that your work is a waiting—and a preparation—for 'socialist practice'?*

As I see it, your question runs the risk of reducing the plural character of subjects by representing them as *tending* towards something singular and full—your question denies the unconscious. However, I accept it and I'll reply as follows: If, in order to live and work, we absolutely need the representation of an end (which, curiously, we sometimes call a Cause), I shall simply recall the tasks Brecht proposes for the intellectual in non-revolutionary periods—*to liquidate and to theorize*. Brecht always couples these tasks together.

Our discourse cannot re-present anything or pre-figure anything. We have available to us only a *negative* activity (Brecht called it *critical* or even *epic*, that is to say, *cut up*—cutting into history), at the end of which shines out, with a distant, intermittent, uncertain light (barbarism always being possible), the ultimate transparency of social relations.

An Interview with
Jacques Chancel
(Radioscopie)

Radioscopie (the literal English equivalent of the term is 'fluoroscopy', a medical imaging technique) was a programme that ran initially from 1968 to 1982 on the French radio station France Inter, before being revived briefly in the late 1980s. It was hosted by Jacques Chancel, one of the best-loved figures in French broadcasting in the latter decades of the twentieth century. Built around a basic interview format, the programme was a daily fixture in the French audiovisual landscape. Most of France's leading personalities were interviewed at some point and many of them made multiple appearances. A number of the interviews, transcribed and suitably edited, were published in book form. This interview, which took place on 17 February 1975, is available in audio format from the Institut national de l'audiovisuel (INA). A written version, 'tidied up' to some extent, was published in *Radioscopie* 4 (Paris: Laffont, 1976; the volume also contains interviews with Régis Debray, Pierre Mendès-France and Valéry Giscard d'Estaing) and forms the basis of this translation.

The footnotes to this interview are the translator's.

Oeuvres complètes, Volume 4, pp. 887–906

JACQUES CHANCEL. There are many, Roland Barthes, who assert that it's difficult to situate you. Doubtless that is proof that you stand out against received ideas.

We may say—while distrusting labels—that you're a sociologist, a writer, a teacher, a critic and a semiologist. There's a unity to your concerns. And there's also, as we can clearly see—and read—some rigour in your approach.

Since 1953, since your first book, *Writing Degree Zero*, you can be said to have embodied curiosity in all its various roles.

We may wonder, then, what power there is, as you see it, in the act of writing?

ROLAND BARTHES. I assign enormous power to the act of writing. But, as ever, the act of writing can assume different masks, different values. There are moments when you write because you believe you're part of a struggle. It was like that at the beginning of my career as a writer [*écrivain*] or author [*écrivant*].

Then, gradually, the truth came out in the end, a more naked truth—you write because you like writing and it gives you pleasure. You're motivated by bliss [*jouissance*]. Which doesn't mean that, in that act of bliss, you don't come across other motivations, other debates or, quite simply, other people.

CHANCEL. Is the act of writing an extension of the act of thinking?

BARTHES. Not only is it the extension of the act of thinking, it is also perhaps inseparable from it. Your question is very important and it may perhaps be rather complicated to reply. We know, in fact, that we always think with language, that we think while speaking, that we speak while thinking and, in the end, that there's no thought prior to the language that's in us. As I see it, thinking is immediately linked to a form that I already visualize as a written form. That's perhaps a little ambiguous, but I tend to think in sentences, not in thoughts. That's perhaps why it's a bit difficult to pin me down, to situate me—I'm not a philosopher, I'm not a thinker and nor am I perhaps entirely a writer [*écrivain*], as the term was understood fifty years ago. I move from thought to sentence and vice versa. Perhaps that's what's a bit difficult to situate.

CHANCEL. What made you want to rehabilitate the reader at this point?

BARTHES. Because there was, first of all, a historical task to perform. Our history of literature and the way we've spoken about literature for a hundred or a hundred and fifty years has accorded a very prominent place to the writer—all histories of literature are histories of writers and schools, and no thought has ever been given to readers. When a theory of literature was being produced, the level of the reader wasn't one that attracted any interest.

It's necessary now to bring the reader in to the question of the bliss of writing—there's no bliss of writing without bliss of reading. Consequently, if there is something like a new theory of literature emerging, it has to take the reader into account.

CHANCEL. When you remind us of Bachelard's remark that 'Writers . . . are only read,' we might ask ourselves: Did writers exist?[1]

BARTHES. Yes, because, ultimately, we are still reading them. We read them in very different historical

---

1 'For Bachelard, it seems that writers have never written: by a strange lacuna, they are only read.' Roland Barthes, *The Pleasure of the Text* (Richard Miller trans.) (New York: Hill and Wang, 1975), p. 37.

ROLAND BARTHES

lights and they never have the same meaning. That is, more or less, how history works.

CHANCEL. We may wonder what sort of a reader you are. Do you read a lot?

BARTHES. No, I don't read a lot. It's rather paradoxical. I could say, superficially, that it's because I don't have the time, as everyone says.

Being precise, I shall say—still speaking from this level of sensitivity and pleasure—that I don't read much, either because the book bores me and at that point I put it down, or because it excites me, pleases me, and at that point I'm constantly wanting to lift my eyes from the page to carry on thinking and reflecting for myself. All those things make me quite a poor reader in quantitative terms.

CHANCEL. You told me one day that literature was on the way out. Was that just a clever quip or is it what you truly feel? Perhaps you think there's a new literature—an anti- or counter-literature?

BARTHES. Literature with a capital 'L' was, for a long time, a veritable institution. I believe this institutional aspect of literature is, if not disappearing, then at least changing profoundly. The evidence for this is that there are no longer at the moment what we once called 'great writers'.

CHANCEL. As you see it, there was Proust . . .

BARTHES. Yes, there was Proust, though he died before I reached adolescence. But, most importantly, there were people like Gide, [Paul] Claudel, Valéry and [André] Malraux. These were very great names that polarized an entire field of cultural activity, of cultural allurement. It has to be admitted that that's not the case any more. There are intellectuals now, professors and people who write, but with a slightly shamefaced sort of status. And that's a kind of force that is definitely undermining the literary institution.

CHANCEL. Was François Mauriac the last of these great leaders?

BARTHES. Yes, in a sense. But there's a man who had a pivotal position, who came at precisely the point of literature's historic break-up and that was Sartre. Because, ultimately, he exerted—and still exerts—that kind of leadership of culture and literature. But since his work defines itself, precisely, as a destruction of the outward show of literature, of literary prose, he contributed powerfully, by that very fact, to the destruction of the literary myth.

CHANCEL. Roland Barthes, you enjoy considerable notoriety among the young and a great deal is written about you. Some people have said to me: 'He's as important as Sartre was in the Latin Quarter days.' Do you deserve that notoriety?

BARTHES. No, I don't believe so at all. And, with regard to the point you make, I'll reject that impression entirely and reply, perhaps somewhat evasively, that it's very difficult for a person to assess the image the public has of them. It's a very difficult thing.

How do you penetrate the mind of the public? It's not very clear. You meet people who talk to you about yourself, but they are always individuals, friends. As a result, it becomes very difficult to have access, oneself, to the vaguely sociological phenomenon you may represent in a society.

I can say that I'm very philosophical about this generally, that I don't concern myself with it too much and that I try to show no interest in my image.

CHANCEL. You are the founder of semiology, the science of signs.

BARTHES. I'm not really the sole founder—you can't found a science by yourself. And maybe semiology isn't a science yet. For it to become so, it would have to be taught in a very consistent way in the universities.

CHANCEL. You teach it!

BARTHES. I teach it in university faculties. I've practised it at the École pratique des hautes études in Paris, which isn't actually a university, but is, nonetheless, a research/teaching institution. It's rather exceptional. I try, then, to do research in semiology, to practise it but not genuinely to teach it.

CHANCEL. What is your thinking on the status of the sign? And, to begin with, what is the sign?

BARTHES. The sign is a historical object. Ultimately, the sign is a sort of notion that appeared in our Western civilization with the Stoics. Since then, it's had a long history of varied definitions, which was very important in the Middle Ages and which has taken on new life and new interest now through the research done in structural linguistics.

Semiology first presented itself as a science that analysed signs and did so, as much as possible, within social life—not separating the sign from its social impact, its social existence—and, at that point, there was a whole series of conceptual analyses to define the parts, the elements of the sign and the play of the sign when it's alongside other signs. In the end, if not a whole science, then at least a full-blown discourse on the sign was born.

But, as always in France, things moved very quickly. French intellectual history is always very rapid and rather passionate—sometimes without just cause. That semiology evolved because it fitted in very felicitously with the surrounding trends of thought, such as Marxist criticism and psychoanalysis. As a result, semiology is now spreading out into other types of research.

CHANCEL. Would someone who'd neglected to read Marx and Freud—or who wasn't mindful of their existence—know nothing about anything?

BARTHES. No, absolutely not. From my standpoint, intellectual history is a succession of waves of different languages. Now, as it happens, Marx and Freud created a sort of break in Western language [*langage*], a break on which we're still wholly dependent. We haven't produced any great change since those days and we're still within what is loftily termed 'Marxian or Marxist, and Freudian epistemology'. It's simply the case that other languages are venturing to deal with a material and a type of thinking that Marx and Freud set in place.

CHANCEL. Is your itinerary that of a humanist or of an intellectual? You are, in fact, very wary of the word 'intellectual'.

BARTHES. I'm not wary of it when intellectuals are under attack. At that point, I feel an absolute solidarity and I am an intellectual.

I think that when intellectualism is said to be 'on trial', then that's a bit of a sham. These are purely mythological 'trials', wholly removed from reality and there's no nuanced analysis of what the place of the intellectual—often a difficult one, as it happens—might be in current society.

So am I an intellectual? Yes, definitely. But an intellectual who's trying to work with and in his language, not in a thinking external to his language.

CHANCEL. You say: 'Every sentence is a commitment and every discourse is a historical commitment.'

BARTHES. Yes and I still think that. That's why the bliss of writing that I alluded to at the beginning is a bliss that's always dangerous because it's fraught with responsibilities. It isn't a purely gratuitous bliss. What you write has effects, and you are, as a consequence, responsible for what you write—and even the form in which you write it.

So there are these two aspects: bliss and responsibility.

CHANCEL. What knowledge-base is needed to decipher mythologies the way you do?

BARTHES. You just need what at a certain point I called 'the structural reflex', which some people have and others don't. There isn't any kind of privilege in possessing it. You have to perceive social or ideological phenomena from the angle of the meaning—that sort of triggering of meaning—they possess. Then at that point, you decode things, but you do so with lots of intuition in fact, lots of passion too, putting your own values into the decoding. You shouldn't have any illusions about that.

CHANCEL. Do you have the impression of being ahead of your times?

BARTHES. Oh no, not at all! I have the impression . . .

CHANCEL . . . of being understood?

BARTHES. Yes! By a certain audience, definitely.

I have a deep conviction that current society is divided in its ways of speaking. There's a division of languages [*langages*]. We speak a common language, which is French. But if we move to the level of what's called 'discourses', which are made with language but aren't merely language, then at that point discourses are divided. And through the common medium of the French language, there are, in reality, very different ways of speaking [*langages*] which don't communicate well. Personally, I'm very sensitive to this division of languages in our society. I know I occupy a very particular sector of the French language and hence I know my limits, both historical and social.

CHANCEL. A moment ago, you spoke of a 'certain audience'. Will we always talk like that: 'a certain audience', 'certain categories of audience'? Will there always be 'the public, the general public, and a certain audience'?

BARTHES. You're on to one of the great problems of our civilization there. Our society is indeed divided. There's still a class division and, as a result of that, a division of ways of speaking [*langages*], even if social styles of speech don't reflect class divisions simply and easily.

Imagine a society in which there'd be a kind of unitary, homogeneous way of speaking. That's a utopian dream for the moment. And perhaps it isn't entirely desirable. Perhaps utopia would actually consist in imagining a society where extremely different styles of speech would coexist without any aggression between them.

CHANCEL. So, who are you? A stimulator of minds? A harbinger of a new science?

BARTHES. It would be very pretentious to recognize myself in these formulas. In reality, I can't ask myself the question 'Who am I?' Don't think I'm sidestepping the question. I can't ask it. It's for others to say who I am. It's for them to pronounce the word on me. It's not really for me. However much effort I make, what I may say about myself will always be false.

CHANCEL. And yet, when you're writing *Roland Barthes by Roland Barthes*, you ask a question and you expect the reader to reply.

BARTHES. Exactly. I offer the readers a certain number of propositions, of semblances, of analytical fictions, but it's clearly up to them to complete this through their reading, to draw these propositions into their reading and hence find for themselves the adjectives they want, as it were, to stamp on the book.

CHANCEL. But if you're writing *Roland Barthes by Roland Barthes*, it's because you're rather wary of other people, in fact. Because a lot has been written about you and you want to set the record straight.

BARTHES. That would be the case if I thought I'd pronounced the truth about myself. But that isn't how it is at all. I tried, precisely, to show that what I was wanting to do was to describe what I call an 'imaginary of writing', a quasi-novelistic way of experiencing oneself as an intellectual character in fiction, in illusion and not, by any means, in truth. As a result, I don't think that, in writing about myself, I took the place of any critic.

CHANCEL. You go about things cautiously, and even seem slightly distrustful of yourself when you write: 'This must all be considered as if spoken by a character in a novel.'[2] We may take the view, then, that you tell the truth at certain points. But you're also free to invent. This is imaginative writing.

BARTHES. Exactly, it's the imaginary—the moment when you produce an idea or a sentence while cleaving to the image you believe others will have of that idea or that sentence when they get to read it.

---

2 Roland Barthes, epigraph to *Roland Barthes by Roland Barthes* (Richard Howard trans.) (New York: Hill & Wang, 2010).

CHANCEL. I know the importance you accord to ideas, to the Idea. But isn't writing about yourself a pretentious idea?

BARTHES. It's a question I was embarrassed about. You mustn't think I wrote this book in a naively joyful way. I was terrified, at the beginning, by what I call the risk of infatuation—something I detest in others and hence in myself. I was very afraid that writing about myself would look like an act of infatuation. And then later on—this occurred to me as I did the work itself—I took the view that, when all's said and done, we now have a general approach to the human subject that's infinitely more complex, more subtle, less dogmatic than in the past, when we simply had a rather banal sort of psychology for talking about ourselves. There's psychoanalysis, for example, which tells us that when we think we're talking about ourselves, or when I think I'm talking about myself, it is, in fact, very much an unknown self I'm acceding to, a self I don't actually succeed in knowing as I speak of it. There's this kind of layering of the levels of the personality that psychoanalysis enables us to bring out, so that speaking about oneself is an undertaking which, under certain conditions that I've tried to observe, isn't an exercise in self-infatuation.

CHANCEL. And, in fact, you say that writing about oneself is 'a simple idea: simple as the idea of suicide'. Is that simple, an idea of suicide?

BARTHES. I think the idea of suicide is simple.

CHANCEL. Suicide is less simple.

BARTHES. That's the nice distinction I was trying to make. The idea of suicide is an extremely simple one. It may come to you at any moment, for something trivial, some minor setback. The act of suicide is something different. And writing about yourself is a bit like an idea of suicide, because you're terrorized by the risk that goes with it: the risk of images, of infatuation, of narcissism and egotism that goes with it.

CHANCEL. Yes, but negotiating the 'I', the 'he', the 'me'—that's the real obstacle race . . .

BARTHES. Yes, those are pronouns I've used.

CHANCEL. And the 'we'?

BARTHES. 'We' shows a great deal of infatuation. It's very royal, the 'We'! I've made use of these pronouns and I've actually explained about that a little. I've used 'he', because it enabled me to distance myself to some extent from what I was saying—and, precisely, to treat myself as a character in a novel.

CHANCEL. And even to poke fun at yourself.

BARTHES. Of course, I tried. I wasn't averse to taking some wry looks at myself.

CHANCEL. For example, 'I lay myself out all around me: the whole of my little world in pieces; at the centre, what?'[3] So, what is that little world? And what is there at the centre?

BARTHES. The little world is precisely all these fragments I've written and gathered in this little book, all the subjects I talk about. In short, all my little obsessions, my likes and dislikes, my ideas. All that is my 'little world'.

CHANCEL. All your doubts.

BARTHES. Yes, my doubts too. Everyone has his own. You think you're at the centre, but then, when you think about it, you can't actually define yourself as someone who occupies a centre. That's what I was trying to say in that sentence.

CHANCEL. There are all the great ideas but there is, first and foremost, the Idea. So this question suggests itself: Will we soon see ideas the way we see objects?

BARTHES. As a general rule, no. They aren't visible. I admit I have a certain visual relation with certain ideas, though that's admittedly a metaphor. I view them—that is to say, I take pleasure in seeing them in their outlines, in the sentence that undergirds

---

3 *Roland Barthes by Roland Barthes*, p. 93. Translation modified.

them, rather as though they were objects. I referred several times in my book to that form of Japanese poem I'm very fond of, the *haiku*. It's a tiny little poem of just three lines, a very flimsy thing that conveys almost nothing, but it has an absolutely admirable precision and delineation. In that case, you can say you *see* the poem, the *haiku*. I often feel a desire to see ideas like that: to see them as delineated, finished objects—coloured too.

CHANCEL. So, what should we do? Die for ideas—but slowly—or live for ideas? Perhaps, for you, 'idea' has another meaning.[4]

BARTHES. No, you live with ideas. We're talking here on a plane that is, after all, the plane of my subjectivity. I think the game demands it.

CHANCEL. The game everyone plays.

BARTHES. The game everyone plays. It is, in any event, the game of this moment we're spending together. In reality, one lives with ideas. One finds enjoyment with ideas and one debates and struggles with ideas. It's a sort of cohabitation that's both adventurous and very pleasurable—and also very responsible. It's a sort of adventure.

---

4 It is clear from the radio recording that the French original here should read *pour vous*, not *pour voir*, as in the printed text.

CHANCEL. What do you think, then, of those people who say: 'I distrust ideas! I have no ideas!'?

BARTHES. I'm sure they're wrong and are doing themselves a disservice. They have ideas, everyone has ideas. And I'd even say that everyone has ideas that come to them from other people. That goes for writers and intellectuals too. Ideas circulate. There's never really any originality. We live in a sort of large-scale exchange, a sort of grand intertext. Ideas circulate and languages [*langages*] too. In the end, the only thing we can do—and claim it as our own—is to combine them. That's more or less how I see things. But you don't create an idea—it's there, it's like a sort of major transaction in a large-scale economy. Ideas circulate and, at a certain point, you stop them, arrange them and edit them, a little bit the way they do in films, and that produces a work [*une oeuvre*].

CHANCEL. Will there one day be a minister of ideas, a ministry of ideas?

BARTHES. I sincerely hope not. Ideas must really remain free. Institutions must never concern themselves with bliss. That's extremely dangerous. That society should cease to be repressive is all we can ask of it. Above all, it must never have anything to do with bliss itself.

CHANCEL. We're talking about ideas. But there's also the fragment, which, as you see it, is a cry, a scrap, a splinter. Is it a bit of something?

BARTHES. It's all those things at once. It's also a somewhat tactical form, because I wanted to embrace a certain intolerance I have towards what I call 'dissertation', by which I mean sustained, coded discourse that can be rolled out a bit like a table-cloth. So, reacting against 'dissertation', I wrote—with a great deal of pleasure—in this very discontinuous, very fragmented way. This also has to do with the fact that I very much like those writers who proceed by fragments, who've produced works made up of fragments, such as Pascal's *Pensées*. Pascal didn't intend it to be in fragments but that is, in fact, how we read it. Nietzsche himself wrote in fragments but in a much more concerted way that carries us with him a lot more.

CHANCEL. Since you like fragments, you should be fascinated by short stories. Those short stories or novellas we are increasingly seeing published, which are fragments of literature, fragments of novels.

BARTHES. I very much like short stories, even though French literature has never looked very favourably on the form. There are, admittedly, [Guy de] Maupassant's short stories and [Prosper] Mérimée's novellas, but, even so, it isn't a literature of shorter forms. I adore Balzac's short stories, for example.

CHANCEL. Reading your latest book, *Roland Barthes by Roland Barthes*, it's noticeable that you're a demanding gourmand and that everything is referred to the body.

BARTHES. Yes, but there's also a theoretical value to that. The body has now become an object central to the concerns of psychoanalysis.

CHANCEL. Do you want to give it precedence over the mind?

BARTHES. No, not precedence. What I'd like is for us to stop talking in terms of a mind–body duality. Yes to that!

The body is very important, then, because knowing it is, in fact, an endless task. Knowing one's body is an endless task. And then the body is also the image others have of you, that image we never ultimately have access to, since we never see ourselves. What we see in the mirror is a frozen object, an imaginary object. Similarly, what you see in a photo isn't yourself. I'd say that the only person who's never able to see MYSELF is ME, whereas others see me.

CHANCEL. There's no showing-off about you. Just a need, an overwhelming desire to know yourself better.

BARTHES. I hope there's no showing off. At any rate, I've tried to employ distancing techniques as often as I've been able. I've tried to keep myself at a distance and not exhibit myself in any self-satisfied way. And, indeed, who would I have been exhibiting? It's always the same problem: Where am I? I, myself?

CHANCEL. All the same, in the opening pages of your book, there's a large collection of photos, a veritable Roland Barthes iconography, and I was surprised that you stopped at your adolescence. You say, indeed, that 'From the past, my childhood is the only thing that fascinates me.'[5]

BARTHES. You're right to pick up on that. There are pictures at the front of the book, but I have to point out that that's the way the books in this particular series—*Écrivains de toujours*—are put together.[6] The books are also called 'So-and-so by Himself' and it was more that tradition I was trying to honour. There are pictures, then, centred on the writer himself and I chose these—I built up a sort of imagery which effectively ends with my adolescence because it's only my childhood and adolescence that still fascinate me. What happened after that? I began to write and at that point I'd say that my body 'left the image behind' and was no longer *in* the photograph—it passed into my writing in

5 This is a reference to the passage in *Roland Barthes by Roland Barthes*, p. 22, but Chancel is misquoting slightly. Barthes actually writes: 'It is my childhood which fascinates me most.'

6 The reference is to the French publication. Barthes adds modestly in the recorded interview that he would never have been so presumptuous as to refer to himself as 'un écrivain de toujours' (a writer for the ages).

a quite other way. My body dispersed itself into the act of writing and there was no need to present it any longer.

We're well aware, since Mallarmé, that the writer no longer has to be treated as a 'great figure', that he shouldn't be presented that way any more. I thought to myself that if I went on providing images of myself throughout my life I'd be giving in to that kind of myth of the 'great literary figure' and that's what I chose not to do. On the other hand, the adolescent I was is a person so strange and distant for me, that I could in fact treat him as a kind of character in a novel.

CHANCEL. That childhood, which affects you most deeply, can follow you into adulthood, then?

BARTHES. Absolutely. I tried to explain this with regard to two or three photos by reading 'the expression, the look' I had when I was a child. I see inner states in them, emotions and patterns of feeling that were already present in me as a child. In that sense, one never grows up—*the body*, to be precise, doesn't mature. And we know very well from psychoanalysis that the emotions, the patterns of feeling of childhood persist and stay with us in adult life and even into old age.

CHANCEL. A first love or a first sadness, a first joy?

BARTHES. Exactly. There aren't just events, there are also states—states of distress or boredom. The mere fact of being bored, the fact of being lost in the world can all be read off from a childhood photograph, whereas you perhaps couldn't do that now from current photos, even though I feel these things are still there within me from time to time.

CHANCEL. Can we say there's an injustice, since you're said to be responsible for your life when you're not responsible for your childhood?

BARTHES. You aren't, in fact, responsible for your childhood, but if it marks you and stays with you, it's never completely done away with.

CHANCEL. When you say, 'Only the images of my youth fascinate me,'[7] we may well ask what was this youth which you refer to also as 'not an unhappy youth but an awkward one'.

BARTHES. I explained that I'd been happy because I was surrounded with affection and, on that very important level, I had all I could wish for. At the same time, I had a difficult childhood and youth, which isn't a privilege, a badge of honour or anything exceptional. I belonged to what might be termed an impoverished liberal bourgeois family. My father, a naval officer, had died in the 1914–18 war and my mother raised me in very difficult financial circumstances. That left its mark on me.

7 *Roland Barthes by Roland Barthes*, p. 3.

CHANCEL. So, for you, it was the time of solitude, that solitude you've delved into a great deal.

BARTHES. Yes, because in reality I had no milieu when I was an adolescent, insofar as I was attached solely to my mother and hers was my only household. The only social milieu I was part of was that of my grandparents, to whom I went more or less as a visitor during the holidays. And so, having no real social milieu, I experienced a certain solitude which was interrupted only by the school friends that you have when you're an adolescent.

CHANCEL. For today's students, you're the man they want to know about. Can we say that the fact that you're famous—or, rather, recognized—is something of a crowning glory?

BARTHES. I think one has to be very simple. It has to be said that 'the fact of being recognized'—your expression's a very good one—is an expression that only had theoretical importance in the days when we were happy to be under the influence of Sartre's philosophy. The fact of being recognized is, in fact, very important—I would even say it is necessary. It makes us feel good and keeps us at our work. It isn't at all a negligible thing, and it would be ridiculous to take a sort of virtuous, Stoic philosopher's attitude towards the recognition you might receive from a particular public or a group of researchers or even intellectuals.

Having said that, it's something that never lasts very long. Gratifications of a social kind can be intense, but they're never very long-lasting, because you're soon reclaimed by the responsibilities of work, by the need to do something else, to move on. At that point, doubts, anxieties and difficulties take over again, which are the normal tissue of our lives.

CHANCEL. Were the health problems you had in 1934, when you were just 19 years old, what set you on the path of serious thinking?

BARTHES. Certainly. The illness I had at that point, pulmonary tuberculosis, an illness which has completely changed character today, struck at a time when it wasn't yet treated with drugs but solely by stays in sanatoria or surgical operations.

I got that illness at a point when the person who contracted it was subject to a very serious taboo, the taboo of contagion. It was, moreover, both a very long and very slow illness, and you couldn't monitor its progress yourself because you weren't actually suffering but felt well. It was simply the doctor who decreed that you were sick and you'd have to live for years with this kind of 'higher medical decision' hanging over you. The doctor decided whether you were ill or cured.

I spent many years at the students' sanatorium at Saint-Hilaire-de-Touvet in the Isère. I also spent time in a Swiss sanatorium. I had two particular experiences there. You really mustn't get the idea that when you're isolated in a sanatorium, you become a sort of solemn thinker. That isn't what happens at all.

The first experience was one of friendship—you live for years with people your age and you often share a room with one or two others. You see one another every day and the deep emotional ties which develop in that milieu—with its joys, its problems and its whole novelistic aspect—gives you enormous support.

The second experience was an experience of reading. What else is there to do but read? It was in that period that I read a lot, particularly French and foreign classics, and that I began to write for the sanatorium's student magazine *Existence*. I read the whole of Michelet's published work, for example, which I worked on later. That was very important to me.

CHANCEL. You say that 'words are social phenomena'. There's a word we don't use any more. That's the word *tubard*, a slang term for a tuberculosis patient, but one that meant more than just that . . .

BARTHES. Yes, it was a very pejorative word.

CHANCEL. It's a word that's happily been killed off.

BARTHES. Happily killed off. That's very well put!

CHANCEL. When you grant words the importance you do, should we trust in them?

BARTHES. Yes! We have to trust in them while retaining the conviction that history will very much kill them off as and when necessary!

CHANCEL. Following what you do, it seems clear that you've moved beyond the sphere of your studies, your literature degree. But you also say: 'I can say that I haven't read Hegel and I'm none the worse for it!'[8]

BARTHES. I didn't say I hadn't read him. I said that you can say this because we live in a cultural world where there's a 'superego'—a pressure that makes us feel obliged to read certain books, so that we'd feel guilty if we hadn't. I simply wanted to push back against that pressure and explain that we very often know books without having read them— there's a sort of cultural osmosis that happens.

We mustn't be slaves to the literal reading of a book. A book has another life than that of the letters that make it up. It comes into conversations and into one's friends' reactions—these too are ways for a book to exist.

CHANCEL. When did you realize you had to write?

8 See *Roland Barthes by Roland Barthes*, p. 100. Again, Chancel's recollection of the book is not absolutely precise.

BARTHES. I wanted to write very early on. When I was an adolescent, I read a lot—Gide, in particular—and I very much wanted to write. Then that desire was put on hold because I felt that the act of writing was caught up in a sort of mythology of rather solemn, inauthentic collective images that no longer matched up to the needs of the times. It was only late in the day that I felt entitled again to manage my writing freely.

CHANCEL. If writing guarantees exchange, how is it with speech?

BARTHES. It's also an exchange, but it doesn't bring the same subject onto the stage in the same way. For my part, I greatly prefer writing to speech. Speech is a problem for me because I'm afraid of theatre—I'm always afraid of theatricalizing myself when I speak. I'm afraid of what's called hysteria, of finding myself drawn into collusive nods and winks.

CHANCEL. Into confessions?

BARTHES. Not really. More into more or less willing seductions. Though it has to be accepted and one has to play the game, in life today I'm afraid of speech.

CHANCEL. You ask this question: 'Where do they [my parents] come from?' You answer: 'From a family of notaries!' And you add: 'Here I am poor. Here I am endowed with a race, a class ... The line ends in a being *pour rien*.'[9] There is something like an end.

BARTHES. It's an elliptical formulation. In this 'being *pour rien*', I wasn't alluding or referring in any way to a genuinely biographical situation. I was alluding to the fact that writing today is an expenditure for nothing, an 'unconditional expenditure', as Georges Bataille would say . . . It's a sort of perverse activity which, in a sense, has no purpose, cannot enter into any kind of accounting and always goes beyond the practical tasks we may ask of it.

No doubt writing's part of a social exchange. When you write books and have them published, it's all part of a publishing market and belongs to a particular economy. But, in writing, there's always something additional which goes beyond questions of economic return and it is the *pour rien*, the 'for nothing' that defines the 'bliss of writing' and is, therefore, a perversion.

CHANCEL. As a child you were often bored.

BARTHES. Yes, a lot.

9 This is not what appears in Barthes's published book or in the translation. There is a slip of the tongue by Chancel, who initially reads the word *pourvu* (endowed) as *pauvre* (poor). For some reason, this was not corrected when the interview was transcribed, though there is no mention of poverty in the relevant passage in *Roland Barthes by Roland Barthes* (see p. 19). For the part of the quotation that is accurate, I have followed Howard's English version.

CHANCEL. Have you been bored as an adult?

BARTHES. As an adult, much less.

CHANCEL. Because you find everything amusing?

BARTHES. Perhaps not everything, but I'm interested in a lot of things, attached to a lot of things.

We always think of a child as someone who can amuse himself. In reality, he's often someone who's bored. I went through that. I was bored a lot in childhood and the older I've got, the less bored I've been. Which means I can say I'm much happier today than when I was an adolescent. This seems rather paradoxical, but it's a finding that anyone who really wants to delve into the matter could confirm.

CHANCEL. For all young people, and more particularly for children, the changes to the body are a discovery. Were you very surprised by the transformation of your body?

BARTHES. I had problems that many people have. To be precise, as an adolescent I was thin and I thought that would always be my body shape.[10] Then, at a certain point, my body changed and when I got over my tuberculosis I began to put on weight. I then experienced a new body, a body that had even

10 In the spoken interview, Barthes also mentions that his lack of weight was why he was exempted from military service.

to battle with a degree of portliness. It's very interesting. There's no more interesting experience
than a slimming diet.

CHANCEL. '[T]o become thin is the naive act of the
will-to-intelligence.'

BARTHES. Yes, I said that. I do believe that can be the
case. For women, it's different—they want to be
beautiful, to be young. With men, too, there can
be a consciousness of one's appearance, but there's
also a desire to be intelligent. We are readier to
believe that lean, emaciated, angular people are
more intelligent than chubby ones.

CHANCEL. Where do you learn to read today?[11]

BARTHES. Let me say that I no longer have the time to
read systematically—and to no particular end. So
I read as my work requires it. When I need to read

[11] The transcription and editing process
seems to have introduced an odd tone into
this question, since the *printed* French version reads 'Apprenez-vous à lire aujourd'hui?'
which literally means 'Are you learning to
read today?' Chancel's words (from the
recording) contain a preamble on Barthes's
love of walking and the Greek saying that
trees are alphabets and he ends by asking:
'Vous, qui avez la science de ces choses, où
apprenez-vous à lire aujourd'hui?' (Where do
you learn to read today?) Barthes's answer
has been heavily 'rewritten' and a subsidiary
question completely excised, all no doubt

certain things for my work, I read and, at that point, I learn.

CHANCEL. You speak of 'The book which I haven't read and which is frequently told to me even before I have time to read it.'[12] We might conclude from this that you know a certain book even though you haven't read it!

BARTHES. I know it because people talk about it.

CHANCEL. So not to read a particular book isn't a scandalous failing?

BARTHES. It's only a failing in a particular sense.[13] If you want to take the *agrégation* in philosophy, you have to have read Hegel.[14] Otherwise, it's no failing at all.

CHANCEL. Though we ought to be wary of the idea of 'duty' in this connection, where does the duty to read begin?

quite intentionally. But 'Apprenez-vous à lire aujourd'hui' seems so odd, in light of the recording, as to be regarded as a mistake and I have restored the missing 'où'.

12 *Roland Barthes by Roland Barthes*, p. 100.

13 In the recording, Barthes clearly says 'dans un certain champ' (in a certain *field*). The transcription has 'dans un certain sens'.

14 The *agrégation*, achieved by competitive examination, is the highest teaching qualification in the French education system.

BARTHES. The problem is one of coming to reading by the path of seduction, bliss and pleasure. There's a social problem in France at the moment, since we're a country where, statistically speaking, very little reading is done . . . But it isn't necessary to force people to read, nobody will get that to happen. We have to reflect on this and find a way to get people to open themselves up to the pleasure of reading. That's what's very difficult.

What I'm saying is a bit hollow, but I don't see very clearly how we can frame the problem on a society-wide scale. It's very difficult.

CHANCEL. As soon as we exclude certain forms of language and writing, we inevitably also banish bodies and we end up saying: 'You don't talk like me, so I'm excluding you!'

BARTHES. Exactly. It's that division of ways of speaking I was talking about. It's something we see confirmed on a daily basis, that certain ways of speaking are excluded. Personally, I've often felt excluded by my language which has been accused of being 'jargon'.

CHANCEL. There's also what you call 'the limpness of big words'.[15]

15 *Roland Barthes by Roland Barthes*, p. 125. Translation modified.

BARTHES. Yes, you can't do without big words, you capitalize them and they become a little grand. In reality, they aren't so grand—they simply stop up the holes in thought. Sometimes thought has holes in it and you put a word in its place. Who hasn't had that happen to him?

CHANCEL. You work so much on your words, sentences and thoughts that political language seems out of bounds to you?

BARTHES. Certainly. It's not that it doesn't interest me. I can even say, in a sense, that I'm passionate about politics but I'm very resistant to political discourse.

CHANCEL. Is there a truth in political discourse?

BARTHES. I don't think so. There may be analytic demands and strictures on it. I believe that the only political discourse that can have value is the one that has an analytical value. [16] That, at any rate,

16 As in the case where 'par rapport à vous' mysteriously became 'par rapport à voir', this sentence seems to have suffered from a serious mistranscription. It is highly improbable that this third sentence of Barthes's reply was intentionally rewritten in the way suggested by the printed text, since not only would the particular sentence make little sense but the meaning of rest of the reply would also be changed beyond recognition (and would strain the bounds of sense to breaking point). I have, once again, followed the recording.

ROLAND BARTHES

is the only political discourse in which I'd be happy to recognize myself and which I'd need. I'd need someone else to produce that discourse for me, but that's all.

CHANCEL. As you see it, writing is ethnology.

BARTHES. Yes, I'm happy to seize on your formulation there.

CHANCEL. Does it explore?

BARTHES. Precisely, it explores! These are images of course, but that seems right to me insofar as the ethnologist, particularly nowadays, is someone who sets off looking not for the 'same'—the identical—but for *the other*. And actually that is what writing is.

CHANCEL. When one's a critic, as you are, it can't be easy to criticize your own work. However, there must be works of yours that you see as having lasting significance. Which are they?

BARTHES. That's a very interesting question and one I've never been asked before. Of my books, I'm fundamentally attached to two. They aren't necessarily the best, as this is a personal, subjective attachment. First, there's the little book I wrote on Michelet, then the one I wrote on Japan, *Empire of Signs*.

CHANCEL. Why Japan?

BARTHES. Because it's a space . . . I don't dare to say a country, since I'm not trying to allude to the economic or political structure of Japan . . .

CHANCEL. But there is a sign . . .

BARTHES. A space, a sign-space, that's both very sensual and very aesthetic. An extraordinary lesson of elegance in sensuality which I find affecting.

CHANCEL. You're director of studies at the École pratique des hautes études. You've conducted an investigation into the voice. Is the voice another writing?

BARTHES. It's still something extremely enigmatic. We tried to work on the voice for a year, and that produced some very good things. Sadly, we didn't make anything of that work subsequently. Perhaps it's a problem we'll come back to . . .

The voice is very enigmatic. It's really the bodily site that's at once the most desirable, the most mortal and the most heartrending, as it were.

CHANCEL. All fields of study have an interest in the voice.

BARTHES. All. Physiology, psychoanalysis, the history of music, perhaps even radiophonic science . . .

CHANCEL. We should also put these questions of voices that are in or out of tune behind us—I don't think that's where the grain of the voice lies.

BARTHES. The grain of the voice has to do with seductiveness and particularly with that presence of the unknown body that underlies the voice and that passes into the voice in a highly mysterious way.

CHANCEL. So, moving from *la voix*—the voice—to *la voie*—the pathway—how do you see the future path of mankind?

BARTHES. I don't assign it any particular path because the concept of mankind is in crisis. It isn't so much the concept of path that's in crisis as the concept of Man.

CHANCEL. You were fascinated only by childhood and adolescence. May we hope that one day you'll be fascinated by old age?

BARTHES. That's a very good question. I am fascinated by old age. In life, I find myself much more affected by old people than by children. Michelet spoke very beautifully but also very gravely of 'This long torture: old age!'

And old age hasn't entered the mythology of our societies. It is repressed.

It's for that reason that it touches me deeply.

For the Liberation of a Pluralist Thinking

Oeuvres complètes, Volume 4, pp. 469–82

This interview with the eminent Japanese academic Shigehiko Hasumi, who was instrumental in introducing French post-structuralist theory to Japan, took place in 1972, the year in which Barthes published his *New Critical Essays*. It first appeared in translation in the Japanese journal *Umi*, published by Chuokoron-Sha Inc. of Tokyo, who are responsible for *Chuokoron*, one of Japan's most distinguished literary magazines. Part of the interview was printed in the French newspaper *Libération* of 16 November 1990, the first full French version having appeared earlier that year in the spring issue of the Tokyo-based journal *Représentation*.

Barthes's book *The Pleasure of the Text*, which is alluded to in the interview, was published by Éditions du Seuil in 1973.

The footnotes to this interview are the translator's.

HASUMI SHIGEHIKO. I'd like to begin this interview by asking you a question about the position you occupy in France, which has for several years now been beset by a kind of *structuralist* fever. The mass media point to you as a representative figure of this new theoretical movement and you're beginning to exert a considerable influence on young scholars. Yet I feel uneasy about this, not because you're a *fashionable* writer, but because, for those who know you from your writings in the 1950s, you're someone who rejects the very notion of influence.

ROLAND BARTHES. Absolutely. That's true . . . I'm grateful to you for such a clear grasp of a question that is, a little secretly . . . in fact, unconsciously, close to my heart. I reject the notion of influence where I myself am concerned and in the way I experience my own life. It isn't remotely that I feel myself beyond certain influences—I could even say which have operated on me—but I would say that if I cast doubt on the notion of influence, it's on account of a certain theory—or, at any rate, a certain ethics—of language.

In reality, I've always experienced the world of inter-human communication essentially at the level of language. That marks me out. Within myself, I can't genuinely put my finger on particular exchanges of ideas or the influence of certain ideas. I can't say that the ideas of a particular man, a particular writer or contemporary, have really left their stamp on me. What goes on inside me is languages or snippets of language. Nonetheless, I could, if you like, say clearly that there have been two men who have, in a general way, affected my work. On the one hand, there's Jean-Paul Sartre, because I came to writing at the point when Sartre was very widely read. He was really the man of my youth—not my adolescence, but let's say my youth—and, as a result, at that point Sartre left a very big mark on me, even at the level of ideas, of general, ideological, moral, philosophical choices, etc. That's certainly the case.

There's another man who had a clear influence on me—indeed I've made no secret of it—and that's Brecht. That's an influence I can situate and specify but, apart from that, if I can put it this way, I'm affected by different languages and I think I have to put it like that because, where the whole semiological or structuralist context is concerned, for example—all the people who are ranged alongside me or who I'm grouped with—though I'm not complaining at all and would be

84 : ROLAND BARTHES

quite happy to feel their influence (this isn't in any sense a question of vanity), it can't really be said that I've genuinely been influenced. What there have been are bits of formulations—it's formulations that come through, do you see? The influence stays at the level of formulations. It's clear, for example, that people like Lévi-Strauss or Lacan have passed on formulations to me. That's beyond any doubt and I don't deny it.

To sum up, it's not by any means in the name of some proud autonomy of the individual that I reject the question of influence—it's exactly the opposite. It's because I believe in what's now called *intertext* and hence am caught up in a network of language and not, ultimately, in a network of ideas. That's how I'd put things.

SHIGEHIKO. Sadly in Japan—and no doubt in France too—you're ranged alongside the Prague theorists or the Russian Formalists.

BARTHES. But that's not something I ever complain about. If some particular paternity or affinity is ascribed to me, then ultimately I never complain. I've no reason to do so, it would be ridiculous. For example, when I wrote my Michelet book, I have to say honestly and for the record that I'd never read a word of Bachelard. Then they said the book was derivative from Bachelard, was influenced by Bachelard, but since Bachelard's someone I admire greatly, and since I very much like what he does, I never complained, you see. But, in fact, it's not true. Once again, I'm only saying all this because—and you know this as well as I do—it connects with a current theoretical problem which is the problem of the *intertext*, which is the question of the wider circulation of languages.

SHIGEHIKO. What's dangerous when you look at things from the standpoint of influences is that you begin to forget to read the texts—your texts, which function like a sort of transformation device, a redistribution mechanism.

BARTHES. Yes, you're quite right about that. And it's a question that interests me very much. This summer, I've just written a little text on the pleasure of the text. I don't know yet whether I'm going to publish it. I've just finished it and let's say I'm not very sure. But I noticed this summer that in this text, which is very short—just sixty typed pages—conversations with friends had slipped in. I can't call this other people's ideas. It's the other people themselves that are there, and I might say, 'I had such-and-such an idea because I spoke with so-and-so one evening' and sometimes I credit other people with ideas I had in their presence. You can see a psychoanalytic theme emerging here. I believe the presence of another person, even when they don't speak but when they listen to you, more or less creates the ideas you have, if

I can put it that way. As a result, influence, as I see it, doesn't at all mean reading authors and then feeling the imprint of their ideas. It's much wider than that, a much larger-scale phenomenon, and in fact it's impossible to pin down.

SHIGEHIKO. What you call a text is precisely this site where these kinds of influences that can't be pinned down are knotted and unknotted. Yet, people prefer to speak of you by listing those markers that can be pinned down: structuralism, formalism, linguistics, semiology, etc. . . .

BARTHES. That's natural, yes. First of all, I did have a phase in my life when for ten years I was, in fact, engaged in those things. That's the point when I was beginning to be known a little. It was the point, shall we say, when I did structuralism and semiology in more or less the proper sense of the terms. That was a para-scientific phase in my life. But it's clear that I've distanced myself from all that a little since then and that what I do today's a bit different. A life is long and you definitely change over time.

SHIGEHIKO. I get the impression that you wrote *Elements of Semiology* as a way of refusing to limit your methodological field and working practice. Was it the same with *The Fashion System*?

BARTHES. Yes, that's very much the case. What you say is very true and I'd say that one writes books in some small measure so as to kill them—so as not to talk about the subject any more. It's a little, very didactic text—it came out of a student seminar—and I think that played its part, because no one was talking about semiology in those days. Now semiology very definitely exists. It's struggling to make headway, but it exists. I think this was a useful book at the time, but you don't need me to tell you that it's already very dated so far as content is concerned and seems very basic as they say, very taxonomic. It's a very rudimentary semiology. It's really a bit like a stained-glass window. It's rather primitive stained-glass window art.

As regards *The Fashion System*, that's really a book I didn't write for publication—I didn't think of it as a product—but as a production for myself. I found enormous pleasure in developing a system without knowing whether I'd publish it or not, do you see? We're talking about the pleasure of the *bricoleur* who tries to build a system. And even if I hadn't published it, it would have absolutely performed its role for me. I hesitated very seriously about publishing it, because I didn't really need to. It was a bit different with my other books because there was writing in them, and hence an erotic game with the reader. But with *The Fashion System*, we're really talking about the presentation of a piece of work. It isn't a product, it's work being acted out in front of other people.

SHIGEHIKO. Here's my first question. It concerns the notion of plurality and I'd like to start from a sentence from Philippe Sollers' recent text on Roland Barthes . . .

BARTHES (*laughs*). Yes, on me. A portrait, so to speak . . .

SHIGEHIKO. He says: 'R. B., on the other hand, lays himself open: meticulous, understated elegance. He arrives on time, is capable of changing his weight quite quickly, bores easily, never seems to be enjoying himself too much, remembers.'[1] And in this sentence, which is both metaphorical and anecdotal . . .

BARTHES. Yes, yes . . .

SHIGEHIKO. You're described as a plural being, but this notion of plurality troubles me insofar as it's just a pure metaphor.

BARTHES. I've often spoken of the plural myself. In *S/Z*, for example.

SHIGEHIKO. Precisely. You utter this word 'plural'. But to speak about the person who is actually the subject of that utterance, the meaning has to be shifted. The French adjective *nul* would be preferable. 'To

---

1 Philippe Sollers, 'R.B.', *Tel Quel 47* (Autumn 1971), p. 19.

arrive on time and quickly become bored', you have to stop *nulle part*—nowhere.

BARTHES. What you say is very true. And very insightful. Clearly, it's always a little tricky to speak of oneself as though one were oneself, isn't it?—as though one existed as a person, as a self. But let's say that if I were a critic and had to criticize myself as an author, I'd stress exactly what you've just said. In other words, in reality, at the existential or neurotic level—I leave it to you to choose—I have one profound intolerance which ultimately governs the whole of my life and work, and that's an intolerance of stereotypes or, in other words, of language that repeats itself and acquires consistency through repetition. I've often spoken about this in asides, though I've never come at the subject head on. In my most recent text I speak about it a bit more. There's the fact that, as soon as language acquires a certain consistency, even if I think it's true . . . the very fact that it's becoming stereotyped triggers an almost physiological language mechanism that I have in me and I react almost with retching and nausea. I can't bear that and so, if I can put it this way, as soon as I feel that a certain kind of language, with all the ideas it conveys, is 'setting' somewhere—the way we talk about mayonnaise or cream 'setting' and acquiring consistency—then I immediately want to be elsewhere.

Obviously, that gets tricky at times. At any rate, it gives me some formidable problems because our current society is very much one that inevitably solidifies certain ways of speaking and writing very quickly (this is a feature of its current alienation) and builds up great momentum around the creation of stereotypes—what I call idiolects, very consistent idiolects—and we modern human beings are, as a result, forced all the time in our lives to move through these ready-made, stereo-typed languages. So, when a language acquires this consistency, I feel stifled and I strive (this is the sense of my work) to try and go elsewhere, even though it's often a language whose freshness and novelty I once experienced and, for that reason, contributed to myself. When it takes on this con-sistency, I want to move elsewhere—that is to say, I become a bit unfaithful to my own language.

SHIGEHIKO. But it isn't really unfaithfulness, it's more being faithful to oneself.

BARTHES. Yes, of course, it's a dialectic. At any rate, it isn't being unfaithful to what we might call major choices of a philosophical, ideological or political type. It's being unfaithful to languages when they become too consistent. As a result, I always have difficulties with the major established languages of the current intellectual sphere—with psycho-analytic language, for example, even though I use it. It's a very consistent language and it's in that respect that it offends me. I also have a problem, which I've no reason to hide, with Marxist language, insofar as, when presented as a vulgate, so to speak, it very much veers towards the stereotypical in places.

Ultimately, everything I write year by year revolves around this theme which is an existential theme because it's a neurotic one. There's also a philosophical resonance to all this, of course: that's where the sort of central sentiment you diagnosed very aptly actually meets up with—and broadens out into—philosophical perspectives. I'm no philosopher myself, but I've definitely been led to campaign theoretically against what's known as monologism, for example—that is to say, against the rule and domination of a single language, a single interpretation of meaning, against the philosophies based on a single, imposed meaning. I've always argued as strongly as I could for the plurality of interpretations, for the absolute openness of meaning, and, if need be, for exemptions from meaning, suppressions and cancellations of meaning.

There again, we're actually in an age that tends very much towards monologism, because it's a highly conflictual age. If we describe it in Marxist terms, we can see quite clearly where the conflicts are and for that very reason it's singular languages, monologistic languages that are doing battle with one another. There's a kind of war of languages and, as a result, in current society a pluralistic attitude is entirely eccentric and heretical. The proof of this is that the Western philosophical tradition is 90 per cent monological. Whether in religion, with Jewish, Christian and even Islamic monotheism, or in secular philosophy, we always find monistic philosophies, and pluralistic philosophies are extremely rare. They're still, let's say, slightly eccentric bodies of thought. So, as I see it, a man like Nietzsche is very important, not as a guide but as someone who actually formulated and freed up a certain pluralism, a pluralist thinking. This is a bit abstract, but I'm sure you can see what I'm getting at . . .

SHIGEHIKO. My second question concerns *Empire of Signs*. The Japanese are always very sensitive about what's written on Japan, but that book shouldn't be read as a study of Japanese culture.

BARTHES. That's clearly the case. I said so at the beginning. I said it briefly but firmly. There's no claim to . . .

SHIGEHIKO. Your intention's clear when you write of the dream 'to know a foreign (alien) language and yet not to understand it—to perceive the difference in it without that difference ever being recuperated by the superficial sociality of discourse, communication or vulgarity'.[2] I think this text perfectly illustrates the basic desire of Roland Barthes or, rather, the *frisson* felt by someone who finds themselves on the fringes of this 'white' writing, this 'no man's land' that you've spoken of so often. For you, Japan was that 'writing degree zero'.

BARTHES. Very right. In fact, that's a theme not of the book in general but of the passage you've just quoted on language. Of course, it's a very paradoxical passage. In practice, it's meaningless to say you love a language without understanding it. What can that possibly mean? But it does mean something for me, doesn't it, insofar as I believe in the existence of what we now call the signifier. I believe there's a powerful erotics of the signifier; that that erotics hasn't yet been thoroughly explored at all, and that psychoanalysis gives us certain means to explore it. But it isn't accepted, particularly by most intellectuals who are, shall we say, a breed of a highly monological cast of mind—you see what I mean—highly dogmatic, and one of the focuses of my struggle is always to fight for the signifier, for its erotic sumptuousness, its drive, its liberation. So, at that point, language—that is to say, all languages in their materiality, not in their meaning or even in their structure in the abstract

2 *Empire of Signs,* p. 6.

ROLAND BARTHES

sense, but everything that relates to phonation, to breath, to the presence of the body in the language—always excites me and more than excites me. In fact, it seduces me, captivates me— in short, it really takes me into the realms of bliss [*jouissance*]. So it's clear that in Japan I was highly, highly delighted, since it's a language I know absolutely nothing of, and when I say absolutely nothing, I mean I can't even recognize roots. It may be that I don't know Portuguese or even Norwegian, but in the street I'll recognize certain words and so on. In Japan, things are totally impenetrable and at the same time (and this is what made me so happy) I was happy to hear the language being spoken, because I could see the bodies in contact with this language that I didn't understand—a whole kind of emotiveness, of rhythms of breathing—and I have to say it gave me daily pleasure, exactly as though I were attending a very fine, very inspiring theatrical performance each day. I have to say it was exactly of that same order.

SHIGEHIKO. I'm probably wrong about this, but it seems to me that you have two books that express a kind of euphoric state—the Michelet book and *Empire of Signs*.

BARTHES. Precisely. You're a very perceptive critic. With the book on Japan, people noticed this, so to speak. People understood that it was a happy book, so it was generally taken that way. But it's rarer to include the Michelet book in this category. I'm going to tell you something that will please you, in view of your insight here. Of all the books I've written, *Michelet* is the one I like best. This is rather ironic, because no one ever really talks about it. It isn't a book of mine that's much discussed— not like *Writing Degree Zero*, for example. For me, the Michelet book is associated with a certain happiness in writing [*bonheur de l'écriture*] and yet, at the same time, there are lots of people who believed I didn't like Michelet. Quite the contrary, it was very much a labour of love. It's a happy book. They didn't see that.

Having said that, it's not easy to repeat ... you can't be happy every year, you understand. It happens from time to time.

SHIGEHIKO. Where Japan is concerned, do you have anything you didn't say in *Empire of Signs* that you'd like to add?

BARTHES. No, in all honesty, I don't think so.

In fact, this commission from Skira ... [3] When I went to Japan, I didn't intend to write about Japan at all. I took absolutely no notes or anything.

3 The French original of *Empire of Signs* was commissioned by Éditions d'Art Albert Skira of Geneva and published by them in 1970.

Several years later, when I wrote this little book, I had to reconstruct things in my mind. Fortunately, I had a few appointment books and that was all. I reconstructed everything and so, to answer your question, I drew out of myself absolutely all that I could in terms of recollections and the retrieval of memories. The book isn't a long one, but I really did bring out everything I remembered about Japan. And beyond that, I don't have anything more to say, because to do so would require me to shift to a completely different level and concern myself with the real Japan. I can well imagine that that would be very difficult to do and I'd be incapable of doing it, at least without going back there.

The only thing I could say is that once I'd written this book of sixty pages of text about a country I was actually in love with (there's no other way of putting it), I understood right away that the Japanese wouldn't recognize themselves in it. I mean I was totally clear-sighted about that from the outset. As a result, I can't say I had the slightest sense of sorrow or regret. But, in spite of everything, I have to say that I'm very conscious it's a book that's not for the Japanese. That's the paradox, do you see? The only thing that can be asked of them is that they understand and accept that I'm clear-sighted about that, and that there shouldn't be any ambiguity whatever about it.

SHIGEHIKO. My third question relates to Flaubert or, rather, to his particular place in your writings. You talked about Flaubert in *Writing Degree Zero*. You still speak of him often, but in an indirect way. It's my impression that *S/Z*, your very extensive analysis of a Balzac short story, revolves around an invisible centre which is the Flaubert of *Bouvard and Pécuchet*. For the sixtieth birthday of Mr Martinet . . .

BARTHES. Ah, yes, you saw that. That line's also in the pocket edition of *Writing Degree Zero* which came out recently . . .

SHIGEHIKO. Right. But it might be said that Flaubert makes himself felt in your thinking not as presence but as absence . . .

BARTHES. I can tell you one thing. There are, if you like, three writers who definitely count a great deal in my life—I might almost say my daily life—in the sense that they form part of my evening reading—not all the time, but I'm always going back to them to some degree. There's Sade obviously, there's Flaubert and there's Proust. So that . . . that kind of selection isn't a selection that's purely theoretical or purely . . . I don't know how to put it. Ultimately, these are authors about whom I can almost certainly say I'll never write a monograph on them. I'll never write a book on Flaubert or a book on Proust. I've written an article on Proust and an article on Flaubert, but these are rather marginal and non-technical articles which focus on quite formal aspects, on problems of style . . . Sade I've written about, but he's the least present of the three, in fact, because the presence of Sade is hard to bear in daily life, whereas Flaubert and Proust are present and particularly, as you said, *Bouvard and Pécuchet*.

So, what's Flaubert to me? If I've not written a monograph on Flaubert, that's precisely because, in reality, I don't have any ideas on Flaubert. I'd be incapable of constructing a critical theory about Flaubert, yet I'm steeped in his work and this is true at every moment, because his work is the very work of writing and, as a result, he's precisely a sort of absolutely pluralized being. As I see it, his is a pluralized work and it comes to me unbidden— it's the direct, manifest *intertext*. There's the turn of the sentences, the gaps between the paragraphs and a comedy too, a certain comedy—well, what he himself called the comedy that doesn't make you laugh. These are entirely avant-garde categories, then, which explain very well why Flaubert, a product, according to the literary his- tories, of a realist age, always seems in reality like an absolutely avant-garde writer. In other words, in the end, everyone and everything that has to do with literature today has a filiation with Flaubert. I'm deeply convinced of that.

Having said this, I shan't, in fact, ever write a book on Flaubert because I've no systematic ideas on Flaubert, I've no critical ideas on Flaubert. Once again, the secret of that is to be found at the level of language and writing. In my opinion, Flaubertian writing (I talk about this in that latest text which isn't published yet. I wrote a short paragraph on Flaubert and I say this there too) is a writing that is, in reality, entirely readable, since Flaubert is a wholly classical author and can be read easily. But, underneath, his is a writing that's at the limits of the readable and also on the verge of a certain madness of language [*une certaine folie du langage*]. It's that whole aspect I find exciting in Flaubert. What excites me in Flaubert is precisely that he's a writer who presents himself as extremely readable with such a kind of existential anxiety about language that I'd say he comes close almost to the conceptions of someone like Georges Bataille. There's all of that in Flaubert, isn't there?

I haven't read Sartre's *Flaubert*, the latest one—I know nothing of that—but as I see it, personally, this is what he is: a sort of great experimentalist of writing. And there's nothing at all abstract about this—it relates to absolutely everyday problems of working. I've a deep affection and admiration for Flaubert's relationship with language—it's an extremely subtle, very sly and not at all spectacular relationship that's very difficult to define.

SHIGEHIKO. At the Proust evening this January at the École normale supérieure, you applied the word 'perpetual' to Proust . . .[4]

BARTHES. Yes, that's right. And that applies to Flaubert too, absolutely. They belong, in fact, among the unclassifiable authors—that is to say, among those who escape the classifications of the literary histories.

I held a seminar three years ago—two or three sessions—on *Bouvard and Pécuchet*. I didn't say much, but I could see that people were very interested. In the end, I don't have anything particular to argue on that subject.

SHIGEHIKO. My fourth question relates to the notion of the 'theft' of language that you spoke of in your

---

4 Barthes explains the sense of 'perpétuel' in his 'Supplement' to *The Pleasure of the Text* (see Volume 1 of this series), making clear that he is not speaking in traditional terms of the 'eternal' value of great literature: 'If the book is not conceived as arguing for an idea or giving an account of a destiny, if it refuses to afford itself depth and anchorage outside the signifier, it can only be perpetual, with no full stop to the text, no last word . . . [T]he perpetual book seems like a book without a project (without argument, without a summary, without will-to-possess)—it isn't going somewhere, it is just going; and it just keeps on going. The perpetual book isn't an eternal book.'

Preface to *Sade, Fourier, Loyola*. You say, 'In fact, today, there is no language site outside bourgeois ideology: our language comes from that ideology, returns to it, remains confined within it. The only possible rejoinder is neither confrontation nor destruction, but theft: to fragment the old text of culture, science and literature, and disseminate its features using barely detectable procedures, in the same way one camouflages stolen goods.'[5] It seems to me that this very fine image of theft stands in a certain relation to 'white writing' [*l'écriture blanche*].

BARTHES. In reality, the idea of the theft of language comes from two key sources: the first of these is an absolutely constant theme since *Writing Degree Zero* and it's in the very title of the book—the 'zero degree' of writing. There's a social alienation of languages [*langages*], even within literature, and hence the dream is to have at one's disposal a 'white writing' that would, in fact, be a writing that wasn't stolen or appropriated—that wouldn't be anyone's property. At the end of *Writing Degree Zero*, I said (said rather than explained, because it's a very assertive, highly metaphorical book) that this white writing doesn't actually exist, that writing is always

---

5 Roland Barthes, *Sade, Fourier, Loyola* (Richard Miller trans.) (Berkeley and Los Angeles: University of California Press, 1989), p. 10. Translation modified.

ROLAND BARTHES

diverted or appropriated in some way and, hence, that writers were condemned, in that regard, to a sort of tragic undertaking, so to speak. So this is still that same idea. Mind you, I've changed a little now, because at bottom I conceive writing [*écriture*]—though, in this case, in the entirely modernist sense of the word—as a space of activity I term *atopic*, that is to say, a space without location and, to a certain extent, without ownership. But at that stage, this writing which is without ownership or place of origin isn't actually consumed by the public. It's an ultra-avant-garde writing, which is an unreadable writing and it is, I believe, very important. It's important that it exists, but there's no clientele for it. Five hundred people read it and love it, but that's all. That's the first idea.

The second—more contingent—source comes from the experience I've had since I've been at the École pratique des hautes études, experience which means a great deal in my life, and from the contact I have with students. Very often when I write now, though I don't actually say so, I draw on impressions relating to my students and a thing I find striking at the moment—and don't like—is that students (well, this is of course a generalization) are very set on developing an ideological critique—they're mad keen on criticizing ideology, hunting it down wherever it is, detecting it, showing that everything's ideological, waging war on bourgeois ideology. It's a programme I've always been committed to myself—for thirty years, if you like—but there is, ultimately, an extremely irritating, depressing side to it, which is that those who do this never ask themselves what ground they themselves are standing on to fight the battle. So, as I see it, my response is what I just expressed here—in other words, there's no language that doesn't ultimately bear the marks of ideology and, as a result, you can't criticize ideology from a pure, neutral ground, a supreme, untainted standpoint, where there's ideological language on the other side but absolute protection from it on your side.

The critical relation, the challenging relation to the other languages of reified society, can only be a relation, not of aggression or destruction (you can never destroy language or we shouldn't talk any more) but of filching and theft, in which you pretend to speak a certain language but undermine it from within. There's a whole technique here that isn't easy to define and there are only qualified successes to be had from it, but I can't see any other solution. In my case, this comes from an ethical stance on culture. I believe that all direct destructions of culture, as postulated in certain forms of avant-garde art or in certain ultra-leftist circles are complete illusions. You never destroy a culture like that. Culture is something else, it's sticky, it's everywhere and you can't do much about it. So there's only one way and that's to cheat. You have to cheat. We need a sort of philosophy or morality of cheating. There you are. It's open to debate, but that's what I think deep down.

SHIGEHIKO. Here, by way of conclusion, is my last question. Can you tell me something about your project on the theory of the bliss of writing [*jouissance de l'écriture*]?

BARTHES. Well, it really seems you have some magical intuitions and premonitions, because, as I told you, I've just written a very short text this summer on the pleasure of the text, a text itself made up of fragments and not at all presenting itself as a theoretically coherent piece. I'd go so far as to say that it isn't so easy for me to talk about it because I've just finished it, but for the sake of simplicity let's say that for several years now my—shall we say, critical—attention has been drawn to this problem of the pleasure in and the bliss of texts. Why is this? For a tactical reason: the development of a theory of writing and literature—let's call it a structuralist science of discourse—has entailed, as always happens whenever there's an attempt to build a science, an extremely purificatory, castrating attitude towards the *eros* or the erotics of reading and writing. The fact is bracketed out that when we read a text, it undeniably either gives us pleasure or bores us—we relate to it erotically.

And no one ever talks about that. Scholarship doesn't concern itself with that, partly because there is, at least in Western culture, a continuous censorship of the idea of pleasure, which is downplayed and undervalued.

For example, we don't, in our part of the world, have any great philosophy of pleasure. Only one man has put pleasure at the heart of his philosophy, a man I have in fact devoted time to myself, and that's Fourier. But he isn't a great philosopher. Everyone regards him as crazy and hare-brained. In other words if we want to think about pleasure, about eros, we people of today, we have no philosophy at our disposal. I'd even say that the only current philosophy—philosophy in the very broad sense—that's taken this problem of pleasure head-on is psychoanalysis. You can't criticize psychoanalysis for not dealing with pleasure. But in reality it has only an extremely pessimistic view of pleasure—it always subsumes the idea of pleasure under the idea of desire which is an infinitely more pessimistic one.

So there was all this—let's call it philosophical—context, the fact that scholarship, particularly with regard to the work of students, stresses in a very superego-ish way—really foregrounding the superego—methodological obligations and attitudes that are often very castrating in relation to texts. There was also the whole business of ideological contestation. I'm thinking, for example, of writings such as those of . . . I don't know . . . the *Cahiers du Cinéma*, which always end up totally castrating the erotic relation to the art work, supposedly for reasons of ideological analysis. I wanted to react against all that by concerning myself with the pleasure of the text, while being aware, nonetheless, that it was dangerous, because, though the pleasure of the text is something that's frowned upon to some extent right across the board, we can say that on the Left, among scholars and protest groups, it definitely meets with censure. Unfortunately, rightists frequently lay claim to it, but they do so for profoundly reactionary reasons. In reality, it's to eliminate politics that people say: 'Give us literature which is pleasurable, that's all we ask,' etc.

At first I situated pleasure in a pluralist, anti-monologistic field and hence one without any ideological superego. I explained that, deep down, one is entitled (I'm simplifying here) to take pleasure in ideologically reactionary texts, and pleasure was no respecter of ideology. Gradually, I was led to apply a distinction which is, in fact, psychoanalytic in origin, between pleasure and bliss. From there, it's possible to conceive that there are texts of pleasure and texts of bliss. Texts of pleasure are texts which are, in general, in the domain of culture, texts which accept culture and, in psychoanalytic terms, refer to it and to the imaginary surface of the self and, hence, to very reconciled, highly pacified zones of the subject. Whereas bliss is always based ultimately on perversion or, to put it very roughly, on a sort of loss of consciousness, a kind of fetishization of the object, a sort of major upheaval—in a word, a very fast-acting trauma.

Those texts that are termed *modern* are generally of the bliss type. The text of bliss doesn't necessarily give pleasure—there may be texts of bliss that give an impression of boredom. I played on these two things. I tried to explain that, somewhat unfortunately for me, I was myself an extremely contradictory man, perhaps because of my past and my generation, because I didn't choose between the text of pleasure and the text of bliss, because I needed both and hence was caught in a kind of historical contradiction which meant that, on the one hand, I often rehabilitated works from the past at the level of pleasure and, on the other, I championed avant-garde works at the level of bliss and that I was, therefore, an anachronistic subject.

I'm doubly perverse because I'm doubly 'split' as the psychoanalytic terminology has it. This is perhaps a little abstract. Things very quickly become abstract when you've just been working on them because you want to sum things up very quickly and . . .

SHIGEHIKO. The trace of this double perversion might be seen in your earliest writings . . .

BARTHES. Absolutely, that's rather clear. Certainly, at one stage in my life I went through a phase myself which I've described as a phase of scientific fantasy. Scientificity functioned as a kind of fantasy for me. That was the time of the beginnings of semiology and it was the point where I was beginning to be known a little. I don't deny this at all. I'm very happy to concede it. Only at the moment I'm very much occupied with a theory of the signifier, of literary erotics. There you are, that's all I can say. Well, clearly that's going to change my image a little . . .

A Meeting with
Roland Barthes

Oeuvres complètes, Volume 5, pp. 735–43

This interview, conducted by Nadine Dormoy Savage, then of Herbert H. Lehman College of the City University of New York, first appeared in French in the *French Review*, the journal of the American Association of Teachers of French, in February 1979 (52[3]: 432–9).

No precise date is given for the interview, but it seems reasonable to suppose that it was made at some point in 1978 or, just possibly, in the very early days of 1979. In 1978, Barthes presented his second series of lectures at the Collège de France, on the subject of 'The Neutral' and delivered on Saturday mornings, from 18 February to 3 June 1978. Later that year, Barthes began his penultimate lecture course, 'The Preparation of the Novel I: From Life to the Work', which ran from 2 December 1978 to 10 March 1979. Both lecture series have been published in English translation by Columbia University Press.

Unless otherwise stated, the notes to this interview are translated from its original publication in the *French Review* (February 1979), though additional information has been added in certain cases.

This greying individual with his reserved manner, impassive mien and even-toned voice, whose speech seeks neither to be assertive, arrogant nor dogmatic and, above all, is not effusive, is one of the most passionate men alive. He has, first of all, a passion for writing, but also a passionate sensibility in his perception and analysis, as witness his latest work *A Lover's Discourse: Fragments* published by Éditions du Seuil in 1977.

At the age of 62, Roland Barthes has reached the peak of his career. Since 1962 he has been director of studies at the École pratique des hautes études for 'the sociology of signs, symbols and representations' and, for a second year, he occupies the chair of literary semiology created especially for him at the Collège de France. His course attracts hundreds of listeners each week, who carefully record his words on dozens of cassettes and innumerable notepads that come from every corner of the known world. To attend his lectures is to experience a special moment situated literally outside of time, in a space where everything is cast into question and yet where everything has its place in the vast panorama he patiently paints with a series of little touches, and where he invites us to recognize our own fantasies or, in other words, our language.

'Modern literature worthy of that name can only be questioning,' he wrote in his *Critical Essays*. His approach continues today to consist in a methodical and individual exercise in the deflation of all our society's myths. The ideologies of Right and Left, each of which secrete their own language, while ascribing a monopoly of objectivity to themselves, are rejected equally by Barthes who has given them a name—the ideospheres. Among them reigns the dominant ideology or doxa, which dreams of order and unity, which confuses nature with custom and reduces the world to an essence in order to immobilize it.

It is through linguistics, structuralist criticism and psychoanalysis that Barthes has demonstrated, throughout his work, the parallel that exists between the stance of the writer towards language and that of the human being towards the world. 'Writing . . . is a blind alley, and it is because society itself is a blind alley.'[1] Hence, for Barthes linguistics is already a philosophy, but it is just beginning: 'Linguistics is at the dawning of its history: language is there for us to discover in the same way as we are now discovering space. Our century will perhaps be characterized by these two forms of exploration.'[2]

We asked the famous author of *Mythologies*, whose intellectual rigour is matched only by his total unpretentiousness, to bring us up to speed, between two weekly lectures, with his current preoccupations.

1 Roland Barthes, *Writing Degree Zero & Elements of Semiology* (Annette Lavers and Colin Smith trans) (London: Vintage Books, 2010), p. 93.

2 Roland Barthes, 'Situation du linguiste', *Oeuvres complètes, Volume 2, 1962–1967* (Paris: Éditions du Seuil, 2002), p. 814. First published in *La Quinzaine littéraire*, 15 May 1966.

NADINE DORMOY SAVAGE. In one of your lectures at the Collège de France, you stated that the problem of language isn't to make oneself understood or to communicate, but to obtain recognition from the other.

BARTHES. This isn't actually a very personal position. It's a position that encapsulates a whole debate, a whole movement of an epistemological nature. Generally, linguists regard themselves as scientists studying communication. Some linguists have asserted this aim of linguistics with a certain arrogance. As they see it, linguistics is forbidden from considering anything that isn't communication. That's the position of a linguist like [Georges] Mounin, for example.

This is an epistemological view that reduces language to pure communicational activity, and all current developments in logic, philosophy and psychoanalysis are actually opposed to that position. Human beings are absolutely consubstantial with language. Language isn't a kind of instrument, an appendage they might be said to possess 'additionally', in order to help them communicate with their neighbours, to ask them to pass the salt or open the door. That's not how things are at all. In reality, it is language that makes the human subject—human beings don't exist outside of the language that constitutes them. Language is a perpetual exchange and no language is monological.

There is no monologue, since even when we think we're speaking alone inside our heads, we are in reality always addressing ourselves in a more or less hallucinatory way to an other—or to the Other who is there and surrounds us. To this point of view (which isn't a subjective position of mine, but actually represents a whole strain of current thinking), we should add that there's the whole of symbolism—in all the richness of that word—in language. The symbolic isn't just a communication activity—it's the realization of the humanity that's in human beings. As for receiving recognition, that means that when I speak, I can't do so without having a certain idea, a certain image of the other to whom I'm speaking, an image of what they're expecting of me and of what they are themselves. I'm trying to foresee how they'll take what I say, how they judge me, etc. And while I'm doing this, I'm judging them myself, and when they're listening to me, they're also trying to conceive the image I have of them and what their silence will mean, etc. Let's say that in languages there's an exchange of images.

For thirty years structural linguistics has taken the form of a strict analysis of the structural facts of language as a combinatory structure of units, and it was necessary for it to do so. Linguists and people interested in linguistics have now very clearly realized that that wasn't enough, and that there was something else in language that we had to begin to study. What is really going on—not just in the abstract—when two people speak to each other? This line of thinking began in Oxford philosophy, certainly, and with the British philosophers who focused their thinking on language.[3] It has been continued in certain forms of logic and also, to a large extent, by psychoanalysis—language as exchange of images and as, effectively, exchange of recognition. When I speak, whatever I'm saying, I'm calling on the other to recognize me. Linguistics must concern itself to some degree with this exchange of places, of places that are clearly implicit, often unconscious and, of course, very difficult to untangle. But it's definitely the case that language isn't just for communicating—it's quite simply for existing.

SAVAGE. The subject of your course this year is 'The Neutral'. In *Critical Essays*, you wrote: 'No one, then, can write without passionately taking sides (whatever the apparent detachment of his message) as to all that happens or does not happen in the world.'[4] Are we now seeing an attempt on your part at withdrawal or disengagement from your earlier approaches?

---

3 The philosophers concerned here are Ludwig Wittgenstein and J. L. Austin.

4 *Critical Essays*, p. xvii.

BARTHES. 'The Neutral' isn't a systematic disengagement or a withdrawal. It's trying to find new—and somewhat original—modes of engagement: a fragmented engagement, a discontinuous engagement, an unexpected engagement, an oscillating engagement. I've talked a bit about all this in the course. Ultimately, the Neutral is what isn't systematic. So a withdrawal that was systematic wouldn't be neutral.

SAVAGE. You described the Neutral as, among other things, the time of the 'not yet', a crossing, suspended time, a mask or a screen against a certain anxiety. It seems to me many people would recognize themselves in this state of mind. Yet you continue, even in the Neutral, to 'take a stand', insofar as you use writing [*écriture*].

BARTHES. No one shakes off that contradiction. No one can really resolve it. I see it in the doctoral theses I supervise. Many of these involve criticizing the ideological character of certain discourses, certain works. And they often hit the mark. It's all very well done and correctly analysed, but when you criticize the ideology of others, you're forced to do so with a discourse which is, ultimately, itself ideological. This produces a sort of dead-end we all find ourselves in. We've a highly sensitive awareness of other people's ideology, but we can't find a language free of all ideology because it doesn't exist. It's my contention that, of all languages, writing—if you will, the work of enunciation based on the literary model—is still the discourse with the least ideology in it, because it's the discourse with least arrogance and least fakery. Writing isn't beholden to truth and is, indeed, consciously accepted illusion—illusion, fiction, art—but, as such, it is, in the end, less mendacious than a discourse that lays claim, dogmatically, to truth.

SAVAGE. Is scientific language a writing like any other?

BARTHES. I shan't call science a writing because I reserve the term for forms of language which, in my own mind, I regard very highly. But the so-called human sciences, as opposed to the so-called exact sciences, definitely need ordinary discourse to express themselves. Now, those sciences never call the language they use into question. They take the view that it's a self-evident language, that it's purely instrumental and they never admit to themselves that they are, in the end, using a discourse that is itself in the grip of ideology and constrained in what it can say. There's a kind of fundamental deception about the science or sciences that claim to be using language merely as an instrument, that don't consider what I would call the hallucinated element of language, to use a term I've already used before. In every discourse there's always an imaginary dimension the human sciences have never questioned—at least up to now.

SAVAGE. You've explained to us, in effect, that every language is hallucinatory since, as it takes its place, it also asserts certain images—that every language has a pathos about it, since it's a continual struggle with grammar, that language is assertive and hence arrogant, that there are things it forces us to say and others it prevents us from saying. In short, you used the word fascism when talking about language. And, indeed, you often use Greek words or neologisms with the accompanying comment that the French language needs 'supplementing'.[5]

BARTHES. I don't have in mind the French language in particular. Supplementing the language is an idea of Mallarmé. As he saw it, writing or literature or poetry serves to supplement the language. The language as described by its lexicon and grammar is something with substantial gaps in it. Subjects feel they can't express themselves through the ultimately rather impoverished syntactic or lexical resources the language affords them and, moreover, as I've often said, the language forces us to

5 The *French Review* article appears to have been mistranscribed in the version of this interview published in Barthes's *Oeuvres complètes* and the word 'grecs' has been omitted. [Trans.].

ROLAND BARTHES

speak in a certain way and stops us speaking in another. For example, there's no neuter gender in French and there are cases where that can be a very great hindrance. I may have nuances in my head which mean that I'll be very frustrated by the lack of a neuter in French. I imagine, for example, that subjects may find it a hindrance that English doesn't have the distinction that French has between *tu* and *vous*, that there's only one form of second-person address. So there are some awkward constraints in language. Discourse, literature— everything you do with the language serves to provide supplements for what the language lacks. My discourse wrestles with language (*la langue*) in a way. On the one hand, it's forced to use language and draws what it can from the language, and at the same time it wrestles with it. That's a very dialectical position. But this is the case with all languages. There's no language poorer than any other. At times, if I feel a French word doesn't fully express what I want to say—being deficient in its connotations or cultural richness—then at that point I use a foreign word—a Greek one, for example—a word that's relatively freer and less compromised by use.

SAVAGE. There are forms of language you particularly distrust. For example, in *Writing Degree Zero*, you write: 'The preterite and the third person in the Novel are nothing but the fateful gesture with which the writer draws attention to the mask which he is wearing';[6] and, with regard to adjectives, in *Roland Barthes by Roland Barthes*, you wrote: '[T]o abolish—in oneself, between oneself and others—adjectives: a relationship which adjectivizes is on the side of the image, on the side of domination, of death.'[7]

BARTHES. You have to make a distinction here. The proper name, the third person, the simple past or preterite are features of novel writing. It was as such that I said I couldn't bear them. Let's say that, if I were to decide to write a novel, I'd be a little embarrassed to use 'he' and 'she' or the simple past and to give proper names to my characters. Why would that embarrass me? Because it's part of a completely threadbare code. So if I used those forms, it would mean I was accepting the code in all its threadbareness. That's not impossible. You could say that you agree to write a novel as it was done in the past, that you accept that. But it raises substantial problems. There's a resistance to certain forms. Where adjectives are concerned, it's quite different.[8] This isn't a problem of novel

6 Roland Barthes, 'Writing Degree Zero' in *Writing Degree Zero and Elements of Semiology*, p. 46.

7 *Roland Barthes by Roland Barthes*, p. 43.

8 In this instance also, I have followed the original text of the interview ('Pour l'adjectif,

writing but a problem of life, a problem of one's relations with others at every moment. Applying an adjective to a human being, even if that adjective is kindly and complimentary, definitely means consigning that human being in some small measure to a sort of essence, a sort of image. As a result, once you reach a certain degree of sensitivity, it becomes to some extent an instrument of aggression. Having said that, this is a very utopian struggle, because you can't speak without adjectives.

SAVAGE. Your way of going about your analyses is highly eclectic. You use quite a number of different approaches?

BARTHES. Yes, I've always wanted to apply new and different languages to old objects. That's how I'd define my critical activity. At certain points I used psychoanalytic language to quite an extent, without being in any way a specialist. I do that a lot less now and, when all's said and done, I hardly do criticism any more. In my course at the Collège de France, you may have noticed that I don't study a particular work. I read works and then bring elements of them into a thinking that isn't actually criticism: it lies elsewhere and is more a kind of ethical investigation—into how we're to behave in

c'est tout différent'), *not the Oeuvres complètes version.* [Trans.]

life, how we're to live. In the end, that is indeed an ethical investigation.

SAVAGE. Have you found it necessary to work a little bit differently at the Collège de France from the way you work in your other teaching—at the École pratique des hautes études, for example?

BARTHES. I've been at the Collège two years. I was the one who wanted the Chair to be called the chair of 'literary semiology'. It wasn't for my own purposes that I wanted the word 'semiology' to be attached to the chair, but in the hope that it might help other semiologists, especially young ones. You'll be aware that semiology isn't recognized as a university discipline and each time a young researcher comes up before a panel or committee with his or her career depending on it, there are difficulties because semiology isn't recognized as a discipline. So I thought that by granting semiology the honour of a chair at the Collège, which is after all a prestigious institution, I'd perhaps help to gain proper recognition for the subject. But, ironically, at the very moment I became professor of semiology, I practically stopped doing semiology at all. I've passed through semiology, I worked for it in its beginnings, but now I regard myself as an outsider who's entirely at liberty where methodology is concerned. As for the audience at the Collège, I didn't know what it was like. I've only had an audience for two years and it's something new to me. This is a real 'public', since anyone can come—you don't have to register. For my part, I couldn't define it. I can see that it's very varied in age and I've a clear sense that there are different cultural levels. As a result, I'm drawn towards a discourse I'd describe as less methodological, less technical—more 'human'.

SAVAGE. Can you talk a bit about your interest in oriental cultures?

BARTHES. Factually speaking, it's absolutely clear that a Westerner can't have genuine access to Far Eastern cultures for linguistic reasons. They're very difficult, very distant languages and it takes years of very great specialization to learn them. And even then, there's no guarantee you'll pull it off. A Western intellectual can't afford the time to do that. Even if he did set about learning a bit of Chinese, it's absolutely clear that after three years of effort he still wouldn't know the language. The same applies to the languages in which Buddhism is couched. So we get only a very vague, very distorted reflection of Far Eastern thought and we Westerners don't put ourselves into a position to reach the truth or acquire a reliable footing where the Far East is concerned. We don't turn towards Far Eastern thinking as though it were a truth, because we don't have access to it linguistically. But the East is useful to us because it represents an authentic otherness. After all, all Western cultures and their religions are ultimately very similar. We can see quite clearly that there are admittedly differences, in the end, between Islam, the three Christianities—the Orthodox, the Catholic and the Protestant—and Judaism, but it's the same form of thought. The East functions, then, as the Other of that thought, and we need (at least it's necessary in my intellectual life) a sort of oscillation between the same and the other. What I'm able to glimpse of Eastern thought, through very distant echoes, gives me a chance to breathe.

SAVAGE. Might the East act as a sort of foil to the spirit of aggressiveness and confrontation that exists to some extent in Western culture?

BARTHES. You can project personal fantasies of gentleness, rest, peace and a lack of aggressiveness on to the East, because the East often lends itself to that. There are many genuine features in Eastern thinking that support such a view.

SAVAGE. Could I end by asking you to say a few words about your new work, which, from what you say of it yourself in the Introduction, is about rehabilitating—if I may put it that way—the discourse of lovers, which is somewhat forgotten today?

BARTHES. Let me make clear that the discourse on passionate love has been abandoned today by the intellectual caste—that is to say, by those who think, who theorize. Lovers' discourse disappeared from the concerns of the intelligentsia a long time ago. That's where there's a 'solitude' of the lovers' discourse, since it is, by contrast, very well represented in popular culture, in films, novels and songs. I was taking the standpoint of the intellectual that I am.

SAVAGE. I've extracted a quotation from your book: 'To know that one does not write for the other, to know that these things I am going to write will never cause me to be loved by the one I love (the other), to know that writing compensates for nothing, sublimates nothing, that it is precisely there where you are not—this is the beginning of writing.'[9] Could you explain this a little?

BARTHES. It's an intentionally rather paradoxical ellipsis which comes at the end of a meditation on the desire felt by lovers to give their writing to the one they love, to make them a present of it, their writing being the best of themselves. Loving subjects want to give this best part of themselves and they gradually discover, in a kind of relatively dramatic deflation, that writing, as it is produced, in fact takes on a sort of consistency, autonomy and opacity that means it cannot reflect that gift. And so it's consigned to a certain solitude. This is my

9 Roland Barthes, A Lover's Discourse: Fragments (Richard Howard trans.) (New York: Farrar Strauss and Giroux, 1978), p. 100.

deep conviction. To take a historical example, let's look at someone who tried to put the gift of love into his writing, such as Heinrich Heine, the German Romantic poet. He always had very unhappy love affairs. He wrote some splendid love poems, yet these love poems never reached the woman they were addressed to. For our part, we find ourselves the beneficiaries of a writing that wasn't addressed to us. That's what writing is—it's a solitude that doesn't reach its goal, but perhaps reaches a goal you didn't have in mind.